Women's Reflections
The Feminist Film Movement

by
Jan Rosenberg

UMI RESEARCH PRESS
Ann Arbor, Michigan

Produced and distributed by
UMI Research Press
an imprint of
University Microfilms International
Ann Arbor, Michigan 48106

Library of Congress Cataloging in Publication Data

Rosenberg, Jan.
    Women's reflections.

    (Studies in cinema ; no. 22)
    "A revision of the author's thesis, University of
Massachusetts, 1979"–T.p. verso.
    Bibliography: p.
    Includes index.
    1. Feminist motion pictures–United States–History
and criticism. I. Title. II. Series.

PN1995.9.W6R63 1983 791.43'09'09352042 83-1271
ISBN 0-8357-1400-4

For Fred

Women's Reflections
The Feminist Film Movement

Studies in Cinema, No. 22

Diane M. Kirkpatrick, Series Editor

Associate Professor, History of Art
The University of Michigan

Other Titles in This Series

Contents

Acknowledgments

This study would not have been possible without the generous cooperation of feminist filmmakers/distributors/organizers who spoke honestly and at length about their personal, political, and professional experiences. Nor would it have been completed without Alice Rossi, whose intellectual guidance and personal encouragement (somehow always in the right proportions) enabled me to delineate the forms and patterns within the chaos of experiences and data I had amassed.

1

Introduction: An Overview of Political Film Movements in America

Introduction: Culture and Politics

Connections between culture and politics are among the most allusive yet significant analytical problems in contemporary social science. The feminist film movement, a self-consciously political and inherently "cultural" enterprise, addresses this problem head-on. The successes and failures of the feminist filmmakers inform us, experientially and analytically, about culture and politics in a contemporary milieu.

To most contemporary feminists, the mass media are held to be particularly effective modern conveyors and even sources of cultural values and ideology. From infancy to adulthood, the feminists argue, parents, teachers, and "the media" bombard girls and women with powerful normative signals which embody and perpetuate female subordination and inferiority. Having internalized these media-transmitted messages, most women then "choose" roles on which the age-old structure of female subordination squarely rests.[1] Although the two main (initial) branches of feminism, "women's rights" and "women's liberation," concurred in their diagnoses of the media, they prescribed different remedies. The "rights" branch emphasized reforming the dominant culture, while the "liberationists" put their energies into creating alternative cultural forms, e.g. feminist magazines, newspapers, and "independent films." (Chapter 2 provides an elaboration of these trajectories, and thus situates the feminist film movement in its immediate political and historical context.)

The terms "independent film" and "independent filmmaker" are ambiguous and somewhat misleading, yet a consensus is crystallizing along lines defined in the most authoritative report yet published on independent film.

The term 'independent' implies that a single individual has primary and unquestioned creative control over the production of a film. To have this control, it is usually necessary for a single individual to conceive the film, to be the primary motivating force in the production of the film, and to control the capital invested in the film. This is true whether the film is a narrative feature, a documentary production, or an avant-garde film.[2]

What is crucial, for feminists and other independent filmmakers, is that the filmmaker conceives the film and also *directs* the production of it. In addition, feminist filmmakers, like other independent filmmakers, may occupy many functional positions in the production crew: cinematographer, editor, sound person, or gaffer (lighting director).

Two caveats are in order in applying the distinctions made by Peter Feinstein in the report cited above to feminist independent films. First, though many feminist filmmakers work individually, a number of women (and a very few men) also cooperatively conceive of and guide the production of their films with one or more equal partners; in filmmaking more than in other arts, feminists have challenged the artistic "imperative" of individual creative control. Second, within this study "independent film" refers almost exclusively to documentary and avant-garde films. Until very recently, feminist filmmakers have not had access to the financial resources required for feature filmmaking.[3]

The rapid rise of the feminist film movement gives us a rare opportunity to explore the shifting tensions and problems inherent in aestheticizing and marketing feminism. If we can understand the historical and sociological connections between feminism and film, including who the filmmakers are and where they come from, the clusters and subgenres of the films, and how markets are invented and routinized, we will have illuminated the conjuncture of politics and culture in an important contemporary movement. First, however, it is necessary to present a broader historical overview of political film in America.

Political Film in America:
The Larger Historical Context

Several historical waves of political films prefigured the ideological, pragmatic, and organizational problems that have plagued the feminist film movement. Film waves documenting public issues first appeared before World War I and have continued sporadically up to the present. In the pre-War period moviemaking was still a new and open industry in which newcomers could successfully make and market movies, which is precisely what some prominent feminists did before the First World War. By the twenties, though, the organization of Hollywood had changed drastically; power in the new industry was already so tightly consolidated that outsiders could rarely produce movies.

Long-forgotten, though recently rediscovered, suffrage movies and movie criticism offer an obvious starting point for this discussion. Several pro-suffrage films were produced by women's movement leaders between 1912 and 1914. These films were attempts to educate and persuade the expanding movie-going public of the suffragists' normalcy and of their just demands. Jane Addams and Dr. Anna Shaw starred in *Independent Votes for Women* (1912); Sylvia Pankhurst and Harriet Stanton Blatch were featured in *Eighty Million Women Want---?* (1913); the final suffrage film, *Your Girl and Mine* (1914), was produced in cooperation with the Congressional Committee of the National Woman Suffrage Association, but apparently did not feature any feminist political leaders.[4] Both of the first two films, by emphasizing the suffragists' "ordinary womanly virtues" and the value of heterosexual relationships, tried to counter the deviant images which repeatedly confronted the women's movement. In 1914 a major review in *Motion Picture World* suggested that *Eighty Million Women Want---?* had done this successfully. It read in part:

> Those who have looked upon the Votes-for-Women movement as the last refuge for old maids and cranks are due for a most pleasant and agreeable disillusionment. The heroine of the story, though a staunch enough suffragette, is womanly from top to toe, and both she and the hero look and act their best when they gaze upon the marriage license which forms the finale of the story.[5]

According to Marjorie Rosen, who has done pioneering research on these films, the suffragists "oversaw all aspects of the production, made sure that attractive women played leading roles, and subversively enhanced their feminist messages by setting them within lively 'acceptable' stories of love and marriage."[6]

Similarly, many of the best-known contemporary feminist films also present moderate, broad-based appeals which implicitly try to dispel popular misconceptions about "radical, man-hating" feminists. In both eras, then, film is used to mediate between the movement and the public and to recruit new members. Within the contemporary movement, however, feminist films also promote intra-movement solidarity and *esprit* and are frequently shown at feminist gatherings.

Film forms and themes also differ in the early and contemporary periods. Early suffragists made explicitly political, fictionalized films which followed the traditional melodramatic film structure of the period. All of the early women's films concern women's political or legal rights. Like the women's movement of their era, they focus primarily on the public, political issue of women's suffrage. By contrast, most contemporary feminist filmmakers, working as "independents" in an alternative filmmaking milieu, make either documentary or avant-garde films which are shown in schools, libraries, museums, and similar non-theatrical settings, rather than fictionalized features shown in standard movie theaters. Feminist documentaries and avant-garde films explore a wide range of public and private issues which preoccupy contemporary feminists.

Although some women reformers (and other Progressives) in the earlier part of this century recognized the emerging power of the movies, unlike their heirs in the 1960s, they did not view women's media image (not they would have articulated it in this way) as a *basis* of sex inequality. Even the astute Jane Addams, while acknowledging the educative and "escapist" potential of the movies, didn't anticipate the advent of their massive influence.[7] Although Addams advocated use of the new industrial art form and even helped produce a suffrage movie, her related goals were narrowly focused on winning the vote for women.

Political films about women's issues did not appear again until the rise of the contemporary feminist movement, but several alternative (non-feminist) political film waves surfaced in the intervening years. These films were made outside of the dominant movie industry, and stood in opposition to the structure of power and privilege in America. By the 1920s the structure of the movie industry had changed considerably from the pre-war period. The movie industry quickly became an enormous enterprise in which power was highly centralized and resources were tightly controlled.[8] By the twenties it was no longer possible for outsiders to produce and distribute movies as Suffragists and others had occasionally done before the War. Political activists and others who wished to make movies now had to work outside of, and in opposition to, the new Establishment; they couldn't afford the most up-to-date filmmaking equipment and could not exhibit their films in regular movie theaters, which the studios owned and tightly controlled.

During the late 1920s some leftist filmmakers, inspired by the legendary practice and promise of the Soviet film industry, organized themselves into a radical filmmaking unit called the Workers' Film and Photo League. This was a self-consciously oppositional left-wing group which viewed its films as vehicles for political organizing. Their founding statement reads in part: "The movie must become our weapon. It must spread the message of struggle against unemployment, starvation, and police clubbings." League members, like the radical filmmakers of the sixties and seventies, felt that the dominant cinematic conventions of fiction films had to be replaced by the progressive documentary form. Even in the twenties, radicals opposed the form as well as content of the Hollywood dream machine. The League's statement continued: "(the movie) must reflect the workers' lives and problems . . . struggle against and expose the reactionary film . . . to produce documentary film reflecting the lives and struggles of the American worker. . . ."[9]

In addition to criticizing the actual movies, members of the Film and Photo League also challenged the traditional audience-film relationship. They repudiated the conventional views of movies as entertaining or educational. Movies were seen as catalysts for political discussion and action. Given their activist perspective, members of the League saw the need for discussions to accompany film showings. The hope of involving the audience in an active way, so important to leftist artists and filmmakers in the sixties, is thus a radical aspiration of long standing.

During the thirties technological changes accompanying the introduction of sound films led to further consolidation of power and control within a few major Hollywood studios. According to film historian Lewis Jacobs, "The vast capital necessary to make a sound film has restricted individual experimentation and has kept the movie in America almost entirely a commercial undertaking."[10] In spite of this, Frontier Films, a well-known alternative political film company, made documentaries and feature films from 1936 to 1942. Left and left-leaning artists of considerable renown such as Paul Robeson, Muriel Rukeyser, Paul Strand, and Leo Hurwitz were core members of Frontier Films. During its short existence this political film group made films on the Spanish Civil War (*Heart of Spain*), on work, unions, and corporate violence in America (*Native Land,* a fictionalized film), and a documentary on a trade union organizing center (*People of the Cumberland.*)

Radical political challenges to the consciousness industry, as well as those to the society in general, were submerged in the 1940s and 1950s.[11] World War II and the Cold War which followed cut the ground from any visible opposition. McCarthyism was especially lethal to leftists in the movie industry.[12] While the political opposition was being decimated, however, important cultural opposition took root. This period marked the origins and the early growth of the avant-garde film in America.

In contrast to the social concerns and aesthetic realism of documentaries, avant-garde films are defined by their personal and introspective leanings as well as by an abstract, experimental aesthetic. The contours of consciousness, sexuality, and emotion continue to preoccupy avant-garde filmmakers. By the late 1960s and 1970s these problems, viewed through the prism of a woman's experience, also preoccupied a great many feminists. In redefining "the personal as political," feminists invited a reconsideration of many daily activites and artistic undertakings once dismissed as "merely personal." Women's intra-familial experiences, diaries, letters, and abstract art (including avant-garde film) were subjected to feminists' scrutiny.[13]

In the United States, the only body of explicitly political movies produced by the dominant industry are those associated with World War II. After Pearl Harbor, pervasive American attitudes of isolationism had to be reversed quickly among military draftees. A series of military training films were produced and widely used to mobilize support among recruits. Popular support for the War effort quickly mushroomed in Hollywood as in the rest of the nation. There followed an enormous outpouring of explicitly patriotic nationalistic movies which were commercially distributed to audiences across the country. In their comprehensive survey of political films, Isaksson and Furhammer describe the production of war movies by Hollywood studios as follows:

> . . . almost its entire output seemed steeped in propaganda. . . . In this enormous offering of propaganda as entertainment, *Hollywood Quarterly* estimated that of the total film production for the years 1942 to 1944 about 375 Hollywood movies had a more or less openly expressed patriotic purpose . . . a majority of the most important directors were also involved in the psychological war effort.[14]

With the important exception of World War II films, explicitly political film waves in the United States have emerged and existed in reaction to the dominant movie culture. The most active period of political filmmaking in America occurred in the 1960s. The development of new, lightweight, relatively inexpensive cameras and synchronized tape recorders during World War II created the preconditions for critical political film movements.[15]

Cinéma vérité emerged as a new film aesthetic in America in the early 1960s.[16] By rejecting many traditional documentary techniques, such as artificial sets, scripts, and dramatic structures, vérité filmmakers tried to "capture life" on film. All American radical film waves in the sixties were enormously influenced by the technological and related aesthetic changes which cinéma vérité embodied.

In America, the single most important group involved in making political films in the late 1960s was Newsreel, a New Left filmmaking and distribution collective. Newsreel, like the Film and Photo League and Frontier Films, was dedicated to loosening the iron grip which the media allegedly held on people's imaginations and political consciousness.

To a considerable degree, Newsreel defined cinematic/political style for the New Left. It was thus very important for the early feminist filmmakers who had been in "the movement." Women (and a very few men) in Newsreel produced several important, widely shown early feminist films. *Janie's Janie* is still among the best known; it is especially important because it established the film portrait as an archtypical subgenre within the feminist film movement. *The Woman's Film,* another early feminist production by Newsreel, also includes portraits of particular women. In *The Woman's Film,* however, the biographical portraits are subordinated to the structural, economic, and political analysis which the film presents. Although the earliest feminist films grew out of the New Left (especially Newsreel), the political and aesthetic directions which the feminist film movement has taken are broader and more eclectic than that now.

Feminist films are part of a unique aesthetic/political movement rooted politically in contemporary feminism (especially the younger, liberationist branch of the women's movement) and aesthetically in independent film traditions as they developed in America. Understanding how the feminist film movement grew out of the women's movement provides a necessary preface to understanding the feminist film movement itself.

2

Feminism and Film

Introduction

Contemporary social critics, and feminists in particular, have been preoccupied with the role the mass media play in shaping social values, institutions, and attitudes. Since the fifties, intellectuals have focused a good deal of criticism on the media; since then most important groups (Blacks, New Leftists, anti-war activitists, women, white ethnics) have included the media in their overall criticisms of the economic, political, and social institutions of American society. To contemporary feminists the images of women and of men in the media and the impact of these images and stereotypes on female identity is a central component in the perpetuation of sexism.[1]

Since the sixties, however, feminists have been divided on their positions toward the prescriptions for the mass media. Some feminists have tried directly to reform the dominant media, while others have produced their own separate, alternative newspapers, magazines, books and films. To explain the origins and development of the feminists' divergent responses to the media, especially to film, it is necessary to refer to the structure of the women's movement. The two main branches of the women's movement, women's rights (the "older" branch) and women's liberation (the "younger" branch) have distinct origins which help account for their overall differences in membership, ideology, organizational structure, program and style. These differences and their implications have been spelled out in great detail by Jo Freeman and Maren Lockwood Carden.[2] Here, it is necessary only to sketch them briefly in order to trace their implications for feminists' media postures. The *women's rights branch* grew out of the mainstream politics of the President's Commission on the Status of Women (established by President Kennedy in 1961) and the State Commissions, formed in the wake of the national commission. Members of the women's rights group were typically "over 30," which has led some observers to designate this as the "older" branch of the women's movement. (The "rights" branch also began earlier than the liberationist branch, i.e. 1966 vs. 1969.) In terms of occupations, most early women's rights leaders were from "the professions, labor, government, and the communications industry."[3] As the women's rights branch developed, it reflected its leaders' backgrounds, ages, and interests and directed its media efforts at changes in the dominant institutions. It has focused primarily on the image of women and the status of women workers in mainstream television, advertising, and the movies.

By contrast, the *women's liberationists* received their political socialization and training in the protest movements of the sixties—the Civil Rights, New Left, and Anti-War Movements. These movements created an ideological framework and personal ties which eventually nourished the incipient women's liberationist movement. "Together these movements created a 'radical community' in which like-minded women continually interacted or were made aware of each other."[4] In style and strategy, the liberationists' media posture bears more resemblance to the sixties protest movements than it does to the women's rights branch. First, their strategy: the liberationists criticized mass culture but rather than trying to reform it from within they tried to create alternative forms to challenge and replace it. Since the late 1960s, liberationists have produced and distributed hundreds of local newspapers, magazines, and films.

Relating to and animating this ideological and programmatic difference between reforming the dominant culture and creating an alternative culture is the liberationists' contempt for "mainstream" politics and their preoccupation with individual creativity and self-expression. Contrary to the official wisdom which holds that the liberationists were more "radical," their radicalism was directed mainly at cultural and personal, not political, targets. While the rights group exerted political pressure on dominant cultural institutions, the liberationists built alternative cultural institutions in order to enhance and provide outlets for their creativity.

Some liberationists attempted to legitimate women's creativity by linking it with feminist values; they constructed a political justification for women's art. All art by women, not just explicitly political art, was seen as a distilled expression of women's underlying structure of consciousness. Women abstract artists pushed this line of argument, seeking to secure a place for themselves in the emerging women's art world. One painter published a polemical defense of women's abstract art in an article entitled "Feminist Abstract Art—A Political Viewpoint":

> In a reactionary escape from formalist criticism, most movement writing on feminist art deals with political issues, but lacks any real understanding of the creative process,

how it functions for the artist and how it affects form and content. . . . Abstract art has become taboo for most artists who consider themselves political feminists. . . . I want to reclaim abstract art for women and transform it on our own terms.[5]

The connections between the feminist film movement and women's avant-garde art are ambiguous, and avant-garde filmmakers are typically ambivalent about defining their films in feminist terms. Rosalind Schneider, one of the few avant-gardists at the core of the feminist film movement, vacillates between discussing her films in "art" terms and in "feminist" terms. Her published descriptions of her films clearly stress their aesthetic, visual dimensions instead of their themes or politics, as the following published descriptions by the author indicate:

"An abstract visual experience designed to simulate a journey into the unconscious;"
"A voyage into red cabbage and shells that transform themselves into the universe;"
"A body portrait of a young woman in relation to landscape and to herself in the tradition of painterly studies of the nude."

Yet when asked if she thinks of her films as feminist, this filmmaker replied, "I feel that they're very strongly feminist in one viewpoint and that is *I deal with things as a woman would see them. . . .*"[6]

The tendency to define women's art as an expression of women's underlying sensibility developed during the 1970s. It provided some justification to include avant-garde films by women at the periphery of the feminist film movement. Anais Nin, a feminist heroine discovered in the seventies, foreshadowed these themes in her diary writings several decades earlier.

This chapter explores the connections between feminism and film in the 1960s and 1970s, with particular attention to the media postures of the older branch of the movement compared to the quite different media postures which the younger branch developed.

Women's Rights and the Movies

The women's rights branch, as has been noted many times before, has focused on reforming the sexist biases within the major institutions in American society, e.g. education, jobs, the law, and the media. From the beginning, members of the National Organization for Women (the first and the largest organization within the women's rights branch) were united and explicit about their mainstream orientation. The NOW statement of purpose, drafted in 1966, made this clear from the start. It reads in part, "The purpose of NOW is to take action to bring women into full participation in the mainstream of American society *now,* exercising all the privileges and responsibilities thereof in truly equal partnership with men.''[7] Programmatically this was translated into efforts to equalize women's education, training and job opportunities, legal and religious status, work and family roles, and even to equalize the images of women and men as a way of promoting the various changes mentioned above. The strategies of the rights branch have reinforced its goals. In pursuit of their reformist objectives, women in the rights branch have often worked through existing legal, political, educational, and occupational structures; this has been as true of women combatting sexism in the media (including, but not primarily focused on, the movies) as in other institutional contexts.

Betty Friedan (founder of the National Organization for Women) and her co-founders worked in the media during the 1950s when the power of the mass media, as well as general recognition of this power, had grown enormously.[8] In the late 1940s and 1950s, the specter of television reintroduced many of the old, early-twentieth-century arguments (as well as some new ones) about the inordinate power the mass media exerts over our collective imaginations and normative order. It was a short step from this recognition of media power to the activists' efforts to gain some control over the content of the mass media.

Betty Friedan's germinal book *The Feminine Mystique* (first published in 1963) is especially significant in defining feminist thinking about the mass media. In *The Feminine Mystique* Friedan identified and provided a rationale and methodology for analyzing the pervasive anti-woman bias in the mass media. She traced the reemergence of the ideology of the lady, which she dubbed "the feminine mystique," in American society after the Second World War. By analyzing the content of popular women's magazines in the 1940s and 1950s, and linking these changes to women's loss of status in the same period, Friedan explored interconnections between ideology and social life. She demonstrated how popular culture could justify and even fuel social change.

Following Friedan's lead and drawing out what was implicit in her book, the National Organization for Women spearheaded attacks on the image of women in the media. Muriel Fox, a board member and early "Chairone" of NOW, is an advertising executive who shared Friedan's view about the crucial role the media plays in attitude formation. Fox urged NOW to take a strong stance vis-à-vis the media, especially advertising. NOW members who worked in the media assumed that the media were powerful in attitude formation, a view not shared in that era by academics and labor leaders. One influential member publicly defined the underlying basis for NOW's emphasis on the media as follows:

I believe that one of the serious battlegrounds upon which the women's struggle will be fought is in the communications media. The stereotyped images of women beamed at us hourly and daily by the newspapers, women's magazines, radio, television, films and advertising are limiting and demeaning and keep us from experiencing our full possibilities.[9]

The NOW national task force on the Image of Women in the Media was one of the original five task forces which NOW established.[10] It has been the most active and influential feminist "media reform" group to date. Midge Kovacs, founder and long-time leader of the New York NOW Image of Women in Media Task Force emphatically recalled the initial mainstream orientation of this committee. According to Kovacs, "Its purpose was to reform the communications media *as they exist.*"[11] I asked Kovacs if she and other committee members knew of, and how they regarded, the independently produced feminist films which women were making in those years; she said that the Image Committee had known of such films but that, from the beginning, there was a consensus among the members that the focus should be on reforming the dominant media, not on promoting women's independent productions.

Kovacs worked for ABC, and her own personal and professional interests dovetailed in two important ways with those that the Image Committee developed: first, the "mainstream" orientation, and second, the emphasis on television. Most other Image Committee members also worked within major (or at least mainstream) media institutions, typically advertising or television. One member who tried to redirect or broaden the Image Committee's direction to include women's independently produced films confirms Kovacs's views. Kristina Nordstrom, a leader/organizer of the women's film movement and director of the First and Second International Festivals of Women's Films, reports that in 1971 she unsuccessfully urged the Image Committee to sponsor special showings of feminist films. She states, however, that at that time she was the only member who was interested in "alternative" films produced and directed by women.[12] My own experiences with the NOW Image Committee as late as 1975 parallel Nordstrom's; my suggestions that we promote feminist films fell on deaf ears.

New York was the only city with a sizeable number of women's films and women filmmakers. In other cities NOW's focus was necessarily limited to mainstream movies because no women's independent film culture existed.

In 1971 the Image Committee developed a television monitoring kit which enabled viewers to document discrimination against women on television. The research which NOW members conducted enabled the Image Committee to mount extensive consumer protests based on well-documented grievances. In 1971-72 NOW led a fight against WRC-TV in Washington (an NBC-owned station) based on the station's employment practices with respect to minorities and women and on the demeaning views of women which WRC regularly televised. The petition included substantial documentation of each point, as these excerpts indicate. First, on the issue of discrimination against women employees:

"There is *not a single woman* listed by WRC as top Management in the 1970 or 1971 Broadcasting Yearbook ...." The following are numbers of women in various union bargaining unit positions which directly affect how women are interpreted to the public:

Job Title (TV, AM & FM)	Female	Male
Network Correspondents	1	19
Local TV & Radio Reporters	3	14
Reporter Trainee	1	0
Local Program Directors	0	7
Local Operations Directors	0	8
News Program Directors	0	3
Film Editors	0	11
Editing Room Assistant	0	1
Stage Managers	1	5
Commercial Film Editors	0	8
Local News Film Editors	0	5
Documentary Film Editors	0	3
Network Newswriters	2	11
Network News Assistants	1	0

The petition concluded with the following statement concerning the image of women:

"Finally, we contend that WRC-TV has violated the Fairness Doctrine by consistently presenting a biased point of view of women's role in society, and by ridiculing or withholding information on the women's rights movement. Today, more than half of all adult women work outside the home. Yet throughout its programming WRC-TV presents the view that the proper and predominant role of women in American society is in the home and that women function and ought to function primarily as wives, mothers, homemakers and sex objects.... We have documented a clear pattern of exclusion from Public Affairs over a 5-month period. Almost 80% of participants were men, and women are rarely portrayed in non-domestic roles outside the home.... WRC-TV's coverage of the women's movement has been biased, and the station has repeatedly withheld or distorted news about the women's rights movement."[13]

Since 1974 the emphasis of the Image Committee of NOW has expanded beyond television and advertising to include the image and employment status of women in the movies and in the movie industry. In the fall of 1974, the New York NOW Image Committee and women in the Screen Actors Guild (SAG) cosponsored a panel discussion and slide show on the image of women and status of actresses. This generated a great deal of interest; hundreds of people (an overflow crowd) poured into a midtown Manhattan lecture hall to hear about and discuss these issues. The outpouring of women led Kovacs to initiate a separate, more narrowly defined task force on the Image of Women in the Movies. One of that group's first actions was at Paramount Pictures; it involved a coordinated protest at an annual stockholders' meeting. A member of the NOW Image of Women in Film Committee voiced criticisms of Paramount's movies and of their personnel practices vis-à-vis women; *Variety* concisely summarized the purpose of the protest as follows: ". . . to question management of Paramount Pictures concerning the company's employment practices and image of women in film. . . ."[14]

During the early seventies, while the NOW Image Committee led the way, other women also became active in researching women's roles and promoting women's interests in the media. *Media Report to Women,* a monthly newsletter dating from 1972, reports "what women are doing and thinking about the communications media and related information." This unusually comprehensive and useful guide to the salient issues and actions concerning women in all aspects of the media includes a wealth of information on women in both the dominant and alternative media, bridging tendencies which are often quite distinct. An invaluable clearinghouse for those interested in women's special status and image in the media, *Media Report to Women* was founded by an economist, Donna Allen, who recognized the media's crucial role in perpetuating discrimination against women.[15]

The most important public event which initially focused attention on women and film was the First International Festival of Women's Films, held in New York in June 1972. The sheer size of the festival astounded most observers. During its 17-day run, the Festival offered 83 separate film screenings. It included movies by major Hollywood and European women directors, as well as a far greater number of independently produced films by contemporary women than anyone had previously known existed. This two-week-long smorgasbord of women's films riveted collective feminist attention (especially that of artists and filmmakers) on films with feminist themes and images which independent women filmmakers had begun producing all around the country. The first Festival of Women's Films, like *Media Report to Women,* included both mainstream and alternative culture perspectives. Part of the difficulties encountered by those women working on the Festival derived from the unresolved tensions between these perspectives. (See chapter 3 for a discussion of this.)

On the West Coast, women filmmakers and media workers were also organizing themselves in 1972. They formed a group called Women in Media in order to publicize their protests and criticisms of the film industry's sexist biases. Like other groups mentioned earlier, their industry-orientation reflected their career aspirations as well as feminist politics.

In Hollywood even more than in other cities, the mainstream movie industry dominated people's conception of film and impeded the development of viable alternative film institutions that might have supported women's independent films, e.g. festivals, distribution cooperatives, and alternative movie theaters that would regularly screen feminist films.

Interest in women and the mainstream movies received more significant national attention in 1973. During that year, three books appeared which critically surveyed the changing contours of women's movie images. Molly Haskell's *From Reverence to Rape* and Marjorie Rosen's more analytical *Popcorn Venus,* both published and widely reviewed in 1973, are the two most comprehensive and best-known of the books on women and film to have appeared by that date. Both survey the entire history of women's movie roles in mainstream American movies and touch on the position of women workers in the movie industry.

Joan Mellen's *Women and Their Sexuality in the New Film* (1973) attempts both more and less than the other two. Mellen's book is much more selective; through an auteurist approach she analyzes the oeuvres of a few very well-known and respected European directors (e.g. Bergman, Bertolucci, Buñuel, and Rohmer) from a feminist perspective. The almost simultaneous appearance of these three books in 1973 both reflected and fostered the growing interest in women's image in the movies. By concentrating almost exclusively on the *dominant* culture (including popular foreign films which, by the time Mellen's book appeared, had become a significant part of the increasingly diversified dominant culture) all three authors reinforced the mainstream tendency and orientation which NOW had been developing since it was founded.

In sum, the rights branch's strategy and posture vis-à-vis the media was consistent with its overall mainstream orientation. It has focused on criticizing the major media, television, advertising, and the movies for their treatment of women. Both the images of women which the media present and the position of women workers within the media industry were examined and found wanting. The rights group had gone on to try to reform the sexist practices and ideology which they uncovered. Rather than producing an alternative culture, members of the women's rights group called for change in the communications media regarding the image of women and the occupational position of women workers.

Women's Liberation and the Feminist Film Movement

While a few feminist films appeared in 1969 and 1970, it was 1971 that marked a real outpouring of the new feminist films.[16] Many were screened for various informal women's groups around the country, as feminist films were becoming part of the liberationist wing of the women's movement. By 1977, at least 250 films were part of the feminist film movement.

Table 1.   Number of Feminist Films, by Year

pre-1969	18
1969	17
1970	14
1971	36
1972	39
1973	43
1974	42
1975	27
1976	14
Total	250

The figures given here for 1976 (and even 1975) are not as reliable as the others. Titles are not likely to show up in distribution as quickly for films completed recently as for those completed several years earlier. In addition, source materials such as printed directories, festival program guides, and entry records from the Second International Festival of Women's Films, are all biased toward earlier films.[17]

The number of feminist filmmakers, like the number of films, has grown rapidly since 1971 when a few women showed their first films. In 1972 there were not more than 30-35 feminist filmmakers; by mid-1976 the number had grown to over 200. The institutionalization of the feminist film movement meant filmmaking was a more visible and viable career alternative for women. In addition, the feminist film movement expanded its boundaries and included filmmakers (avant-gardists) and films (especially film portraits and avant-garde films) not previously considered feminist.

Women are a relatively larger proportion of alternative independent filmmakers in the United States than in any other country. Not only is the women's movement larger and more institutionalized here than abroad, but independent filmmaking is also a far more significant part of the cultural/educational scene in America than elsewhere. Equipment is fairly accessible, skills are relatively easy to acquire, and a number of regular distribution outlets exist to support independent (feminist) films.[18]

A number of different factors help explain the transformation of a few scattered individual women's filmmaking efforts into an identifiable, coherent feminist film movement: the ideological legacy of the "parent" organizations of the New Left; the intersecting issues of age, generational experience, and opportunity structure; and the changing ideology and social base of the women's movement.

The younger, liberationist branch of the women's movement began within the protest movements of the middle and late sixties and maintained an oppositional stance. Seeking to promote social change by creating parallel (alternative) structures outside of the dominant institutions, sixties activists designed alternative families and communes, alternative schools for students from nursery school through college and beyond, and work and consumer alternatives which they instituted in various cooperatives and collectives. Separate, alternative communication organs were designed to diffuse the new knowledge and values among movement adherents and to serve as recruitment nets to those not yet in the ideological fold.

The New Left was continually preoccupied with the politically conservative role of the mass media and the progressive possibilities for alternative media to shatter the media-engendered acceptance of the status quo. New Left theorists engaged in endless analyses of culture and the media, trying to devise effective critical responses to the ever-expanding mass media. They expressed their opposition to the media in hundreds of small, local newsletters, in magazines, newspapers, a national press service (Liberation News Service), a few national magazines (*Ramparts* was the most successful), and film production and distribution groups (Newreel, American Documentary Films).

One of the founders and major spokesmen of New York Newsreel summarized that group's analysis of and response to American society and media this way:

> The subject population in this society, bombarded by and totally immersed in complex, ostensibly 'free' media, has learned to absorb all facts/information relatively easily. Within the formats now popularized by the television documentary, you can lodge almost any material, no matter how explosive, with the confidence that it will neither haunt the subject population, nor push them to move—in the streets, in the communities, in their heads. . . .
>
> We want a form of propaganda that polarizes, angers, excites, for the purpose of discussion—a way of getting at people, not by making concessions to where they are, but by showing them where you are and then forcing them to deal with that, bringing out all their assumptions, their prejudices, their imperfect perceptions.[19]

Like their forebears in the New Left, women's liberationists poured a great deal of energy into producing their own, separate alternative media, mainly newspapers, magazines, and films. This occurred for several reasons. Because of their political experiences, liberationists were already embedded in alternative communication networks. They had greater access to the alternative communications media which had developed in the New Left, e.g. underground newspapers and alternative publishers, than they did to establishment media. Because of their ages (usually "under 30"), they had far more experience with non-Hollywood, "homemade film," both in the underground film movement that took root on the campuses in the sixties and through filmmaking skills which were more widely taught on college campuses in the sixties than ever before.[20]

Liberationist media surfaced early and proliferated quickly; there were only two liberationist periodicals in 1968, but by 1973, 83 had been published.[21] Film production began a bit later and also grew rapidly, though more slowly than printed material due to the scarce resources and expenses involved. Nine explicitly feminist films were completed and screened in 1971; by the end of 1976 over 250 films had been produced.[22]

This move toward film was certainly not a concerted strategy within the younger movement; as Jo Freman indicated, the younger branch was not only decentralized but "structureless," and this precluded the organization of collective political action.[23] None of the "pioneer" feminist filmmakers initially knew of each other's projects. Though they worked independently, they were united by shared political understanding of their film projects. Most of them had been active first in the New Left and then in the feminist movement, and their filmmaking efforts grew out of cultural/political ideas about the media and women that they had formed along the way. (Those not active in the New Left were sympathetic to it.) All of the initial filmmakers had been in women's consciousness raising groups, an experience which each respondent reported was central to the development of her film. The crucial point is that the early filmmakers were moved primarily by social and political, not aesthetic impulses.

Ideological divisions within the liberationist tendency of the women's movement were apparent in the early films. Within the younger branch of feminism the main early schism was between "politicos," who viewed social class divisions as central to all inequality (including women's), and "radical feminists" who viewed the problems of women *qua* women as the crucial ones.[24] Following from this, the politicos' emphasis was more structural, the radical feminists', more psychological and biographic. Although the politicos' dominance in the women's movement was short-lived, they defined the first phase of the feminist film movement. This was largely because of Newsreel's pro-politico position. As the best organized and most effective New Left film production/distribution group, Newsreel produced and actually distributed feminist ("politico") films earlier and more efficiently than individual filmmakers were able to do.

(Typically, the initial feminist filmmakers had enormous difficulty distributing their films. See chapter 5.)

Three of the feminist films finished and screened in 1971 were produced by Newsreel. Two of them, *Janie's Janie* and *The Woman's Film* enjoyed great popularity and wide distribution from the beginning.[25] They both advance familiar "politico" themes; they focus exclusively on the plight of poor and working-class women, on their subjects' emerging feminist/"politico" consciousness, and on their eventual political response to the conditions of their lives. Interestingly enough, neither of these films was made because of leadership or pressure from feminists within Newsreel. *Janie's Janie,* funded by the New Jersey Board of Education, was initially to have been a film about "progressive elements" in the white ghetto of Newark, but the Newsreel crew was unable to find such "elements" among poor white men they met. When the crew members (women and men) met Janie they eventually decided to make a film about her. Having just heard about the structure of the San Francisco Newsreel film, *The Woman's Film,* they decided to concentrate on Janie rather than going ahead with their initial idea—intercutting pieces from a number of different women's lives.[26]

San Francisco Newsreel was barraged by requests from their constituency for a film about women. *The Woman's Film* was clearly a response to these pressures. According to Judy Smith, one of the co-makers of *The Woman's Film,* "There were no women's films and everyone was calling for a woman's film. . . . People would call the Newsreel office and say, 'Do you have any women's films?' So we had to decide what was the next film to make and it was clear we would have to make a women's film."[27] At that time San Francisco Newsreel was less aware of the importance of feminism than its constituency was.[28]

The women's movement changed considerably during the 1970s. Within the women's liberation branch of the movement, the tensions between the New Left's "external politics" and the radical feminists' "personal politics" were resolved in favor of personalism. Biographical issues superceded structural ones; issues of identity and interpersonal relationships came to the fore. The women's rights groups adopted feminist analyses that once earmarked the liberationists, the mass media took over many consciousness raising functions which "c.r." groups had once served, and the women's rights branch absorbed/incorporated much of the women's liberation branch. The women's rights branch became, in effect, the new feminist movement.[29]

The unification of the women's movement has led to an increasingly diverse membership and a broader based and more accepting consensus on traditional aspects of women's lives, e.g. marriage and motherhood.

The mid-1970s election of Eleanor Smeal, a housewife, as President of NOW, is broadly taken as the public symbol of this change which has, in fact, been in the making for several years. A number of the more recently produced films sympathetically explore the parameters and problems of traditional relationships and roles.

Feminist films now reach more members of the expanded women's movement. In the earlier, more polarized era the films were isolated by being shown largely to groups within the younger liberationist branch of the movement, reflecting the younger members' politics but also their greater interest in film, especially independent, non-Hollywood film. Younger women grew up during the time when European and other non-Hollywood films captured the imagination of many Americans. They saw film as the medium of our time—it offered unique possibilities for both political communication and self-expression. Older women still regarded the written word as *the* vehicle of political discourse. It seems plausible that the influx of younger women into the "older" branch of the movement has created more interest in and support for films there.

At the same time, support structures were forming which facilitated the wider distribution of feminist films. Filmmakers and other feminists organized distribution groups which could reach out to the larger, broader feminist market then surfacing. As in other arts, "Women with common concerns get together to provide mutual support both in their work and in their encounters with the establishment, and to share resources, experiences, and ideas. . . ."[30] For filmmakers "mutual support" included feminist film distribution coops, women's film festivals, and collectives of filmmakers working together to make films. (This is discussed fully in chapter 5, "Inventing and Routinizing a Market.")

By 1973–74 the feminist film movement incorporated new types of films which expressed emergent feminist values and themes. The most important and popular feminist films produced in 1974 were personal, biographical and autobiographical portraits of women.

Portrait films focus primarily on one woman. They are about a particular woman at a particular time, often an older woman or someone whose changing status has made her identity problematic. (Several are autobiographical, others feature close relatives, and some protaganists are unrelated to the filmmaker.) In contrast to issue films, the focus of these films is not on women as such, or on a particular social problem confronting women, but on the particularity of a specific woman, chosen for her special appeal and her unique qualities. Although the protaganist may dramatically indicate her individuality and strength of character in response to typical female problems or dilemmas (e.g. divorce, becoming a mother, job discrimination) the film focuses on her strength in responding to a difficult situation, not on the contours or extent of the problem which provoked the response. In *Woo Who May Wilson,* for example, May Wilson's rejection by her husband of 35 years is the background for her life on film. Their break is the occasion for her move to New York and her related personal changes are the subject of this film. She is presented as a woman who is becoming increasingly self-sufficient, competent, and assertive. May Wilson is depicted as "a strong woman." More than anything else, personal qualities of strength and independence define the women in the filmed biographies. Some of the most memorable protaganists are older women with very strong identities and often equally strong senses of purpose—women who made difficult and/or determined choices which often went against the grain of social convention and expectation.

Feminism has led to the rediscovery of female predecessors. Women searching for their "female roots" derived strength from those whose lives they witnessed on screen. Many women were trying to incorporate feminist principles in their personal lives and looked to strong, older women for models.[31]

The film portraits were widely distributed to enthusiastic audiences and received accolades in the feminist press. An editorial in a major feminist art magazine polemically proclaimed the importance of documentary portrait films, comparing them to avant-garde films by women:

> Rothschild's presentation may not be as intricate or as many leveled as Rainer's but it records the beginnings of a new level of awareness rather than documenting the death throes of an old ongoing struggle. *Nana, Mom and Me* is a huge reservoir of source material from which Rothschild and many others, including myself, have and will continue to draw inspiration. Her film gives validation to an area of our lives we, as women, have been brought up to believe is trivial and unimportant. Along with *Antonia Brico, Nana, Mom and Me* is a great aesthetic and feminist statement.[32]

Another feminist critic responded similarly, though more diplomatically, by comparing women's contemporary portrait films to the personal avant-garde cinema of the forties.

> Whereas the films of the forties were poetic—highly symbolic, and imbued with Freudian overtones, the more contemporary autobiographical films are closer to essays—less abstract, more natural, spontaneous, and leisurely. Rothschild's films are also part of the growing body of women's works which constitute a special category—the autobiographical documentary. Unlike pseudoautobiographies such as Jim McBride's *David Holtzman's Diary* and Stanton Kaye's *Brandy in the Wilderness,* the women's films expose the true identity of their makers. . . . These works also are efforts to come to terms with being female.[33]

Film portraits were produced by a number of women who had pre-viously made issue documentaries, as well as by women who had not made feminist films before. (Rothschild, Ashur, Anderson moved from issue to portrait; Bank, and Bonnie Kreps made first films which were portraits.) Personal changes in the filmmakers' lives and statuses, espe-cially becoming or thinking about becoming a mother, or the death of one's mother, prompted a more introspective, personal view and redefi-nition of "women's issues."[34] This trend coincides with the widely felt privatization of American life which so many commentators have noticed in the seventies.[35]

By 1974 the feminist film movement even claimed many women's avant-garde films, but feminist audiences and critics were more skeptical of these. Women's creative self-expression has been an important aspect of contemporary feminism and has legitimized a broad range of women's artistic efforts in quasi-political terms. Avant-garde films by women, like women's poetry, fiction, and painting, are considered by some feminists as important expressions of women's consciousness. The fact that they were made by women, rather than their themes per se, explains the ten-tative incorporation of these films in the women's film movement.

Even as portrait documentaries were pouring forth, some filmmakers and critics were looking for new fictionalized directions for feminist films. They argued that women had taken personal filmmaking as far as they could. Most documentary filmmakers I spoke to wanted to make feature films, and many have already written scripts and/or applied for foundation support for new, larger projects. Amalie Rothschild said:

> I think with *Nana, Mom and Me* I pushed to the limit how personal one can get in documentary form without really intruding on privacy. I think that perhaps the only way to go further is through fiction where you're not dealing with real people's lives and real tensions.[36]

In the words of one critic:

> The time has come to take the insights yielded by these documentaries and enlarge upon them, to create imaginary worlds with fictional characters and boundaries, and revelations for which the filmmaker rather than the interviewee is responsible.[37]

What began as a dissident political/art movement circle is struggling to become a new "establishment"; feminist filmmakers now seek distri-bution for their films on television and in special theaters, and they write fictionalized scripts in hopes of making feature films. Breakthroughs in distribution for films like *Antonia, Union Maids, Hester Street,* and *Har-lan County* raised the expectations of many feminist filmmakers. All four of these films have been shown in carefully selected theaters in major cities and university towns; all received national critical attention and achieved considerable success by any standards, none of which would have been possible without the films, audiences, or support structures which constitute the feminist film movement. If the majority of feminist filmmakers have their way, the feminist film movement will function to provide them with training and experience which ultimately will allow them to become feature filmmakers (directors and scriptwriters) in Hollywood.

In sum, changes within the larger feminist movement are visible in the filmmakers themselves and in the changing themes and styles of feminist films. The following two chapters focus on these issues. In chapter 3 the shifting political and occupational orientations of feminist filmmakers are considered within the contexts of feminism and of the filmmakers' own lives. Chapter 4 presents an in-depth analysis of the major film types in relation to feminist ideology; a preview of that discussion was offered here to foreshadow and introduce some major threads and tensions which tie feminist films to feminism and to the worlds of independent film and commercial movies. The fifth chapter delineates the institutionalization of the support structures which routinize and perpetuate the feminist film movement, and link this movement to other aspects of both feminism and film.

3

The Filmmakers

Introduction

This chapter will present a profile of the feminist filmmakers, focusing on who the women are who have produced documentary and avant-garde films, films which visualize the issues, concerns, and yearnings of women viewers and of the women's movement. The major sociological focus is on linking occupational identities and careers to the filmmakers' backgrounds (social class, educational, and artistic), ages, generational experiences, career paths, and their political, artistic, and personal aspirations in the filmmaking world.

Occupational identity is a crucial and complex aspect of a person's "master identity." This has long been the case for men, especially artists and professionals, and is increasingly true for women.[1] As that part of one's social identity deriving from one's function and status in the occupational structure, occupational identity constitutes a major focus in the life of an adult. Occupational choices and identity have implications for most other aspects of a person's life; they situate one in the class structure, for example, thus defining one's material level and cultural milieu, one's life chances. The discussion which follows focuses on the personal careers of feminist filmmakers. It delineates the various routes by which feminist filmmakers came to their occupations and occupational identities, differentiating the experiences and career paths of older from younger, and of documentary from avant-garde, filmmakers.

Documentary and avant-garde films represent two major kinds of alternative, independent films. *Documentaries,* are films which *treat reality* either by directly recording actual events or by indirectly reconstructing them. They are frequently concerned with social problems for which they may suggest solutions. The popularization of lightweight camera and recording equipment since World War II greatly changed documentary film approaches. The quest for authenticity, as instantiated in direct interviews with spontaneous (unrehearsed) subjects, dominated documentary filmmaking in the post-War era. In contrast, *avant-garde* (or "underground") films are essentially *artistic* creations, typically conceived and made as aesthetic statements by individual artists. The American cinema avant-garde has its roots in subjectivism and continues to be preoccupied with the exploration of the self.[2]

Filmmakers typically pursue a single genre of filmmaking throughout their careers. One woman, Lois Tupper, who began making documentaries with a partner (Maureen McCue) in 1972 was working by herself on an avant-garde film in 1976. She was the only filmmaker in this study who alternated between these disparate filmmaking genres. All others have been *either* documentary or avant-garde filmmakers, a pattern paralleling that found in the larger film world. It is apparently more compatible with one's values and tastes for an avant-garde filmmaker to move from one art medium to another (e.g. painting, sculpture, poetry) than to shift between avant-garde and documentary filmmaking. In part, the filmmakers' earlier interests and orientations determined the kinds of filmmaking which they initially became involved in. Those most interested in social and political issues were far more likely to make documentaries, whereas those who defined themselves primarily as "artists" tended toward the avant-garde. Their occupational identities crystallized as their early self-definitions and orientations were reinforced by the public reputations of their films. Thus, the values which predominated in the filmmakers' originally chosen film world and the "significant others" with whom they interacted or toward whom they oriented their work constrained them to remain in the original genre.

For those who came of professional age before the rise of feminism and the feminist film movement, these distinctions between the two main film/filmmaker types were closely related to differences in the filmmakers' occupational, political, and artistic orientation. Before discussing these key differences, let's turn to a brief description of the population and sample of filmmakers and to a consideration of some broad socio-cultural factors which characterize them as a group.

By the end of 1976, about 200 to 225 women had made one or more feminist films. This figure is based on printed directories of women's films and filmmakers,[3] festival entries, and information gathered from several years of observing participants in the feminist film movement. A sample of 30 filmmakers, or about 15 percent of the total population, was drawn for in-depth investigation. The sample is divided among documentarists (20 filmmakers) and avant-gardists (10) to reflect the approximate distribution and relative importance of these two types in the feminist film world.[4]

Each sample filmmaker participated in an open-ended interview pertaining to the following areas: occupational and educational history and entry into filmmaking; family background and values in relation to art; political orientation, especially concerning feminism; changes in filmmaking concerns as related to personal and political changes; future career goals and ambitions. Most of the interviews lasted between two and a half and four hours, and in many cases they were supplemented by previously published (and some unpublished) material.

All but two filmmakers initially selected for this sample were eager to participate in the study. They welcomed an opportunity to discuss their backgrounds and future goals and some clearly hoped that studies like this one would enhance their legitimacy and visibility. Two documentarists, one older and one younger, were so elusive that interviewing them became impossible. Both of these women were cordial and seemed interested during our initial telephone contact, but they cancelled so many appointments that they were finally replaced by two corresponding filmmaker types. The final sample consisted of 30 filmmakers.

In summary, the findings and analysis are based on in-depth interviews with 30 filmmakers, supplemented by extensive participant-observation, and by published articles and features stories on feminist films and filmmakers.

Class, Family, and Education

Over 50 percent of feminist filmmakers come from upper-middle-class backgrounds.[5] The filmmakers' educational backgrounds provide further evidence of the privileged, affluent surroundings in which they were raised. Fifty percent of them attended elite colleges such as Smith, Brandeis, Vassar, and Barnard.

Some of the specific reasons why filmmakers tended to come from upper-middle-class backgrounds were suggested by the filmmakers themselves, and other, more general explanations have been offered by sociologists who have studied various art worlds. In particular, class-related educational and cultural experiences as well as affluence itself seem to have been important in orienting talented young women toward art and especially toward film.

The middle-class origins of most artists in modern society have frequently been noted. Cesar Grana cites the middle-class social origins of "foot loose intellectuals" in nineteenth century Paris, and Rosenberg and Fliegel's study of abstract expressionist painters in the 1950s in America confirms that, to a great extent, artists still originate within the middle class.[6] The feminist filmmakers are largely *upper* middle class in background, a fact that may be accounted for by the characteristics of filmmaking itself. The training period requires substantial outlays of money, certainly greater than what is needed in painting, sculpture, graphic arts, or even photography. Cameras, tripods, film stock, and processing are all very expensive; even experienced, successful filmmakers who consistently make profits on their films must have the cash or credit for the initial outlay.[7] Novices, of course, have little hope of realizing their initial investment and must be able to sustain financial losses for quite some time before realistically expecting their careers to "take off." As independent, documentary filmmaking has become more professional during the last decade, the training period has become lengthier and even more expensive. This has further restricted the field to those aspirants who have the financial resources to undertake a long and costly training program for a risky, highly competitive artistic occupation. In addition to the actual outlays of money, the training period means that a young filmmaker must forego the possibilities of substantial current income during this period; the total of unrealized income plus the direct costs of the equipment and training program make this a very expensive pursuit with uncertain rewards.

In writing about the differential impact of class background on art students he studied in the 1950s, Mason Griff noted the importance of the middle-class students' privileged position and, by contrast, the limitations imposed on working-class students by their financial obligations to their families. Having to find a job to increase the family income "may mean renouncing a promising future in art."[8] By contrast, the feminist filmmakers frequently reported that their artistic interests were carefully nurtured by supportive parents who did not expect them to contribute to the family income. Like most people who become filmmakers, these women were typically from well-to-do families who could afford to forego their daughters' financial contributions and could contribute to their daughters' material support during their years of training.

A good example of the significance of financial wherewithal is seen in the life of Jan Oxenberg, whose family's status improved markedly during her late adolescent years. Oxenberg realized herself that a change in her family's financial position made a difference in the range of vocational possibilities which she perceived and in the financial support which she could draw on in pursuing these possibilities. When asked how she began making films, she responded by explaining that she was from a working-class family and had gone to public schools.

I never had any access to equipment so I never really thought about it (filmmaking) as a possibility. . . . Well, my parents, they started out being like lower-middle-class and now they're upper-middle-class.[9]

Her family's improved finances allowed them to send her to an expensive graduate school which specialized in the arts, where Oxenberg easily transferred her earlier interests in "creative writing and political work" into feminist art and film.[10] Jan Oxenberg recognized the links between her interests in "political work" (she was active in the educational reform movement of the late 60s), her parents' improved financial position, and the availability of "film culture" and filmmaking equipment at graduate school.

> I definitely recognize that it's easier for me to do what I'm doing (making films) because I have that support; you know, if something happens I can call them. The resources are there, one way or another. It is a privileged position, no doubt about it. . . . Because film is so expensive, I think a lot of people don't even think of getting into it if they don't feel like they know where they are going to get the money to make their first film. Even if they can get grants afterward.[11]

By contrast, another filmmaker had early exposure to art and film because her family was able financially to send her to private schools in the lower grades and high school before sending her to an elite, innovative college (Antioch). When asked, "Had you been interested in the arts when you were in high school?" she offered the following comments:

> Yeah. . . . I went to progressive schools my whole life. So all of that cultural stuff was always around me. And also the whole idea that you could do whatever you want. That I could go make this film without knowing anything about making movies. *I had the confidence that I could go do what I wanted.* . . . I took pictures and made movies.[12]

Another woman whose father is a well-to-do investment banker and who attended a private boarding school also commented on the positive influence which her schooling exerted on her interests in the arts. To the question, "Did your family nurture your interests in the arts?" she responded:

> I'm not consciously aware of my family nurturing my interest in the arts but the kind of girls'-school-type education that I had certainly fostered that. The art part of the women's movement is very much a privileged class kind of thing.[13]

After attending boarding school, this filmmaker went to an elite university (Stanford) and then on to Boston University film school.

These three cases typify the upper-middle-class backgrounds of many of the filmmakers in the study. Their comments suggest that connections between class background and filmmaking derive from the cultural as well as the material dimensions of social class.

Class and Film Culture

Taste in film is linked to social class. As movies and film culture became more diversified in the 1960s, movie audience tastes became more stratified by social class. According to Richard Schickel, movies have been cut off from their traditional mass audience and are becoming a part of high art.

> They are the playthings of the New Class. . . (which) means there has been a fundamental reordering of film's place and function in our society.[14]

Schickel is referring to the new claims and definition of "film" (as opposed to "the movies") as a serious intellectual and artistic form. Herbert Gans supports Schickel's arguments: Gans discusses the differentiation of popular and high culture in terms of class-related "taste publics" and "taste cultures." Like Schickel, Gans notes that foreign films gradually gained a considerable following among intellectually oriented upper-middle-class viewers.[15] These foreign films became a part of the semi-serious cultural fare of sophisticated culture consumers. When the filmmakers were asked about their previous knowledge of and involvement with film, a surprising number of them talked exclusively about the pantheon of foreign films and film directors which emerged in the 1960s; e.g. Bergman, Godard, Truffaut, Fellini, and Buñuel. The following remarks are typical of their responses:

> *JR:*   Are there any film influences that you think are especially important?

> *Martha Coolidge:*   In the early 60s I saw all those European films and I just loved them. Bergman, Truffaut, Godard, Fellini, . . . I loved them all and they were all very, very different. . . . In a sense the only conscious influence on *Not a Pretty Picture* (Coolidge's most recent film) is Godard. . . , he's very shot conscious, and structure conscious; he puts interviews in. He is conscious of the actors as actors, but also as characters, too, because you can't just let them talk. . . . But American (movies) I never saw much of, except those that toured the art theaters.[16]

And another woman said:

> *Ashur:*   My parents were middle class, sort of Jewish intellectuals and we went, you know, movies were important.

> *JR:*   Were you into TV?

> *Ashur:*   No. Not at all, we didn't have a TV. I didn't know much. I went to France and spent a summer at the Cinématecque [few inaudible words] but I really didn't know what I was looking for or at. *I love Jean Luc Godard.*[17]

During their early years the filmmakers knew a good deal about the foreign film "greats," but they were almost totally ignorant of the alternative film traditions in which they would eventually work. Documentarists knew little of, and cared less about, the major documentary filmmakers and movements which preceded them. Two of the three older filmmakers who began as apprentices to leading cinéma-vérité documentarists admitted that they had not ever heard of cinéma vérité and would have preferred working in the "real movies" (meaning Hollywood fiction movies) but the only jobs they could find in the early sixties were in the fast-growing world of vérité film.[18]

Before they became filmmakers most younger documentarists were just as ignorant of their predecessors; those with film training were much better versed in feature film traditions than in "independent" ones. Documentary filmmakers connected with Newsreel, of course, were the exceptions. They had more experience with documentary films, from those they had helped make to those which they saw or distributed (e.g. Cuban and other "third world" films) as part of their ongoing involvement with political film and social change. One Newsreel member, Geri Ashur, explained that her films were heavily influenced by her film viewing and editing experience and by her politics, and that they were made in *conscious opposition* to American educational documentaries. She elaborated this point in talking about *Janie's Janie* by noting the militancy which the film projects, a quality scrupulously avoided by most educational documentaries which strive to present balanced, neutral accounts of their subjects. Like other radical social critics, Geri Ashur discounted "value neutrality," regarding it more as ideological obfuscation than as actual even-handedness.[19]

Like the documentarists, the avant-garde filmmakers who talked about film influences in their early years typically mentioned well-known European directors like Fellini and Truffaut. Suzanne Baumann revealed the electrifying and decisive impact which a Fellini film had on her: "I went to the movies one Saturday night on campus and saw *8½* and . . . I walked out of *8½* and I knew what I wanted to do."[20] Prior to this dramatic turning point, Baumann had been torn between several very different career choices, a scholarly career in philosophy, on the one hand, or a career in fine arts. Filmmaking appeared to her to be a way to resolve the conflicting tugs toward intellectual/conceptual work and artistic expression.

The avant-garde filmmakers cited an important additional source of artistic inspiration. Most of them began as artists in other art media, and they identified much more closely with aesthetic traditions in their initial medium (e.g. painting, dance) and with the twentieth-century avant-garde than with their cinematic traditions. Those who knew some avant-garde film history were familiar with those filmmakers whose reputations were made primarily in art areas other than film, e.g. Cocteau, Genet, Dali. (Connie Beeson, Gunvor Nelson, Freude Bartlett, and Storm de Hirsch all mentioned some of these well-known giants.) As Gans and others have indicated, these interests and enthusiasms are clearly a part of upper-middle-class culture.

A dancer who became an avant-garde filmmaker denied the importance of avant-garde film influence in comparison to her dance background and experiences. In response to the question, "Were you a fan of Hollywood? of avant-garde films?" she said emphatically, *"No, I knew nothing."* To exemplify the limits of her knowledge of avant-garde film and to further demonstrate how mundane her knowledge of film was, she added: "I knew European films, Bergman, Truffaut." She clearly did not regard the filmmakers she named as crucial inspirations or influences. She spoke much more, and more enthusiastically, of her dance teacher's formative influence on her ideas of movement and form.[21]

In sum, it would seem that social class and educational background act as filters for artistic aspirations and activity. The symbolic/cultural and the material dimensions of social class expose women to art and then reinforce their artistic strivings which become occupationally relevant to some. As Hughes has noted:

> The career includes not only the processes and sequences of learning the techniques of the occupation but also the progressive perception of the whole system and of possible places in it and the accompanying changes in conceptions of the work and of one's self in relation to it.[22]

The changes in and diversification of the mass media in the 1950s and the romance of the upper-middle-class with foreign films in the 1960s, helped to establish the importance of film as a serious, legitimate artistic pursuit, especially among the young.

In personal terms, upper-middle-class status generates a sense of financial security which allows women to undertake high-risk careers in which they expect to invest more resources than they earn for (at least) the first few years. Potential filmmaker aspirants from working-class (and even middle-class) backgrounds tend to be screened out of the potential filmmaker pool because they lack the financial resources even to try such a risky venture.

Although alike in class background, the filmmakers interviewed vary significantly in terms of age, generational experience, and the related occupational choices which they faced, choices infused with changing aesthetic and political meanings.

Age and Generational Experience

The feminist filmmakers who took part in this study range in age from their early twenties through their fifties, but the majority are in their twenties and thirties. (See Appendix A for a sample listing of filmmakers by age and film type.) Their youthfulness reflects the recent ascendance of film culture and the relative ease with which younger women interested in politics and the arts have moved into filmmaking since the mid-sixties. (See chapter 2 for a discussion of the broader relationship of generational experience to film.) In addition, there is a very close relationship between the filmmakers' age and the type of film she makes. Documentarists are, on the whole, younger than the avant-garde filmmakers. Fourteen of the 18 documentary filmmakers are "under 35" as compared with 3 out of the 10 avant-garde filmmakers (roughly 80 to 30 percent respectively).

Whether a filmmaker had formal training in filmmaking as part of her educational background is also largely a function of her age. The younger the woman, the more likely she is to have had formal training, reflecting the rapid growth of film studies and courses in colleges and universities in the late 1960s and the 1970s. Eleven of the 19 younger filmmakers went to film school, and 4 of the remaining 8 included some study of film production in their undergraduate or graduate years. Two others entered filmmaking via industry jobs (one in television, one as an editor), and two began making films without any prior training or filmmaking experience, as direct expressions of their feminist politics. Both of the latter two, interestingly, began within the supportive context of collective feminist filmmaking efforts. Judy Smith worked as a member of the San Francisco Newsreel collective on *The Woman's Film* (1971). (Although she was a member of Newsreel, this was the first film that Smith had ever made.) Susan Kleckner was a coordinator of *Three Lives* (1971), the early feminist film organized and edited by Kate Millett. In total, 15 of the 19 younger filmmakers formally studied filmmaking in college and/or graduate school, compared with only 2 of the 11 older filmmakers. (In percentage terms 80 percent of the younger to only 20 percent of the older filmmakers had formal training.) It is almost as likely that younger feminist filmmakers have had some formal training as it is that older feminist filmmakers have not. The older filmmakers began their careers quite differently from the younger ones. Rather than formal study, they were more apt to begin "in the industry" (e.g. in television or as apprentices to established filmmakers) or by producing their own small films. The latter course was far more practicable for women who made avant-garde films, which are typically much cheaper to produce and frequently involve only minimal use and organization of props, crews, and subjects. Film historian Sheldon Renan estimates that such films frequently cost less than a thousand dollars to produce.[23]

It is revealing to contrast the careers of older women who began making films in the early and mid-1960s, before the spread of feminism, with those whose professional lives began later and were, from the outset, influenced by contemporary feminism. This comparison between older and younger filmmakers points up important generational differences in their motives, training, and opportunities as well as the effects of a changing political climate on their filmmaking careers.

Older Filmmakers: The Documentarists

The cinéma vérité movement was in ascendance in the early 1960s and offered intellectual and creative excitement to would-be filmmakers. Even those who had not previously heard of it were quickly swept up in the enthusiasm which it generated once they became involved with this pioneering subgenre. One filmmaker who accidently stumbled into her first film job with the cinéma vérité group expanded on this theme. Her response sheds light on the coincidence of opportunity and accident which landed the early documentary filmmakers in the midst of the cinéma vérité enterprise. Nell Cox explained her own occupational beginnings as follows:

> . . . so then I came back to New York and decided to get a job . . . and I just happened on to Leacock—Pennebaker. Which was just starting the whole cinéma vérité type thing. I was very lucky.
> [*JR:* You just sort of stumbled in there?]
> Yeah. I mean I came to New York because I wanted to make movies and I got a job. . . . The day I came in they had just gotten back from South America. They were just starting a film and they needed people. That winter ended up being really the year when they turned out about 10 films, I think. And so I was fortunate in going from one film to the next. And it was the year that they really developed the whole cinéma vérité thing. So it was a very lively place to be just from the point of view of discussion of documentary film, and what is documentary film? We would sit around and talk for hours. We thought that *we* were revolutionizing . . . the way documentaries were made. And there's no doubt that *they* were.[24]

Cox's shift in pronouns, from "we" to "they," indicates her own marginality within the cinéma vérité movement. Although she saw herself as a serious filmmaker-in-training, the men in charge continued to regard her and the other attractive young women assistants they repeatedly hired, more as decorations than as colleagues.

This theme is more explicitly taken up by another vérité trainee of Cox's era, Joyce Chopra. She expands on the crucial training and employment role which cinéma vérité played, especially for young women, in the early 1960s. Chopra's experiences confirm that aspiring women filmmakers who launched their careers in New York in the early 60s, striving to become the Fellinis or Truffauts of their generation, were far more likely to end up as assistants on cinéma vérité documentaries than as directors of feature-length fiction films. This was not because of their interest in documentary filmmaking but because there was a well-organized and budgeted film group which provided entry-level employment and training opportunities to novices. As Joyce Chopra makes clear in the following account, she "wanted to make movies" (meaning the "real movies") but the only job she could find was with the cinéma vérité group. Chopra unexpectedly had an interview with a prominent vérité filmmaker, David Pennebaker, who introduced her to one of the films and to the overall goals and ideas of cinéma vérité. Much of his introduction apparently passed her by, however:

> I hardly had ever seen a documentary in my life. *I didn't go to make documentary films; I wanted to make movies.* But I wasn't getting anywhere. I had no appreciation of why he [Pennebaker] was so excited and thought it was so special. I just didn't know what documentaries had traditionally been like.

She goes on to talk critically about the role of women apprentices in cinéma vérité, further illuminating their marginal and ambiguous position:

> The other people who were working there at the time in my capacity were all women. We were all apprentices. There may have been one or two guys. . . . But the women were all hired for their attractiveness. I was at a conference recently with Pennebaker and he was describing to a group of sociologists how you make a film and he said, "You know, a cameraman goes out and his girlfriend takes sound." And that sums up that mentality. The way I got to do *Happy Mother's Day* [a vérité film which Joyce Chopra took sound on and coproduced in 1963] was he got some nice young woman he knew, me, to take sound. Which, when you think about it, is ridiculous. I'd never taken sound in my life, really. I kind of knew how to do it. But I would never hire anybody on that basis. But he wanted a nice girl to go out with him to Aberdeen, South Dakota. . . . I didn't think much of it at the time. I doubt that Nell Cox did either.[25]

Women artists, like other women professionals, have traditionally been beset by contradictions and dilemmas in status like those illustrated above. Their professional commitment and seriousness is questioned simply because they are women, and they are often blocked from particular avenues of mobility and success. But the sexist personnel hierarchy and values, and the accompanying social-psychological implications of status contradictions, had ironic outcomes. The women vérité filmmakers all became influential feminist filmmakers in the 1970s, when they transposed their skills and experience into the new film movement and aesthetic.

The underlying assumption and aesthetic of cinéma vérité films, like the personnel hierarchy, were at odds with feminist tenets and film practices as these later developed. Film critics and filmmakers alike have defined the aesthetic of cinéma vérité as one based on "crisis" or "conflict." In their search for an artistic form for the material of everyday life which they were filming, vérité filmmakers selected situations in which a clear conflict was present and organized the film around the resolution of this basic conflict. The dramatic structure of the film was to be found in the actual resolution of a crisis. As Stephen Mamber put it, these filmmakers:

> . . . . saw the crisis moment both as the ultimate goal of shooting and the conclusion of the story. One kept filming until the crisis moment came, and then the story had an ending. This was a pragmatic structure, because the sequence of events in the finished film could correspond to the chronology of filming. The filmmaker would be 'recreating reality' by acting as a witness and then not juggling events out of sequence or deliberately falsifying the record of his experience.[26]

Unlike contemporary feminist filmmakers, who usually select their topics because they are sympathetic to them, male cinéma vérité filmmakers were assigned topics by their sponsors over which they apparently had little veto power. Consequently, the vérité filmmakers were often indifferent and occasionally quite hostile to (as well as ignorant of) their subjects. Compared to feminist filmmakers, they were disdainful, cold, and manipulative toward their subjects.

For a variety of reasons, cinéma vérité had dried up as a coherent movement by the late 1960s. While many of its innovations and impulses have significantly influenced subsequent documentary and fiction film, profoundly altering these forms, cinéma vérité did not remain a viable, coherent film movement. In response to this, as well as to broader socio-political changes, its followers searched for new film forms. For the women, the feminist movement suggested important new themes and approaches.

The three older documentarists who began their filmmaking careers by working on cinéma vérité documentaries have all become influential feminist filmmakers. In 1970 two of them completed their first "proto-feminist" films. Nell Cox completed *A to B,* a vérité-influenced, scripted film about adolescent life in the South, viewed from the perspective of a 17-year-old girl. Madeline Anderson finished *I Am Somebody,* a documentary about a black heavily female strike as seen from the perspective of, and narrated by, a very appealing woman organizer. Neither of these films was intended by their makers as a "feminist statement," but both of them promulgate feminist values and they have been widely interpreted as "feminist films." Cox and Anderson have both become more involved with the women's movement since they made their films in 1969, and both of them encourage the feminist interpretations of their films for ideological as well as financial reasons. In their recent work their more conscious feminist positions are apparent. Both filmmakers portray strong, appealing female characters, Cox in a fictionalized account of a frontier woman (*Liza's Pioneer Diary*, 1976) and Anderson in a documentary portrait of a very old black woman painter, *Clementine Hunter-Artist*.

The other cinéma vérité apprentice, Joyce Chopra, tried her hand at independently producing feature films when she left cinéma vérité but returned to documentaries in 1971. Neither of the two features which she produced expressed feminist ideas, though the one that was adapted from a Thomas Mann short story concerned subtleties of interpersonal, intra-familial relationships which Chopra has pursued in her subsequent work. (During our interview, she contrasted this focus with the crisis structure of the vérité group.) The other film was about a rock group. Unlike Cox and Anderson, Chopra's first feminist film was intended as such: *Joyce at 34*, her autobiographical portrait, appeared in 1972. Since then she has made three other feminist documentaries (*Matina Horner*, 1974; *Girls at 12*, 1975; *Chlorae and Albie*, 1976.) All of these were financed by outside funding agencies, which accounts for Chopra's prolific output. Each film involves themes and approaches which are closer to the ideology of the women's movement than to the aesthetic of cinéma vérité. They all regard their subjects with admiration and accord them respect, and they have no apparent, overarching dramatic structure which "organizes" (or distorts, one might say) the miscellany and small moments of everyday life. Having recognized the disjunctures between cinéma vérité and her own interests and values, Chopra has purposefully and thoughtfully developed an aesthetic built on her feminism.

Anderson, Cox, and Chopra have all redefined themselves as "feminist filmmakers."

Older Filmmakers: The Avant-Garde

The experiences and careers of the old avant-garde filmmakers are quite different from those of the older documentarists. There is an important continuity between the personal/aesthetic roots of the avant-garde filmmakers' initial and continuing motives and interests. The seven older avant-gardists' career choices had much more to do with aesthetic considerations and interrelationships among the various arts than with their desire to become filmmakers. All seven of these women were heavily involved in other art forms before they began making films, and nearly all of them talked about the *formal* appeal which film held for them, about the ways in which it allowed them to explore more fully shape, movement, and spatial relationships. One woman typified the formal interests which led her to filmmaking as she spoke of her transition from journalism to photojournalism to filmmaking.

> I got tired of just writing; I wanted to see the things illustrated. I got a Rolliflex. . . . And I started doing pictures and portraits of friends . . . and then [I got] into photojournalism. And then I started wanting to see the stills animated. . . . Actually the first film I ever did was stills, all stills.[27]

Another woman, a painter turned sculptor turned filmmaker, spoke of her involvement in several new media in terms of light and color. For Rosalind Schneider, painting gave rise to a strong interest in form, which later led her back to explorations of light and color. Her earliest sculptures were styrofoam carvings which she eventually illuminated from behind, and her interest in the manipulation of light led her into filmmaking. When she began making films, she realized how much she had missed color as a sculptor and introduced this into her films.

Storm de Hirsch, a filmmaker who started out as a poet, spoke eloquently of the complementary difference between her poetry and her filmmaking:

> I never dreamed I would get into film. But there were times when there were no words for something I wanted to say, and there was a feeling of wanting the words to leave the page and get into action and become something else. This was the case with . . . *The Tatooed Man.* It was originally a poem, but it was a poem that particularly had the feeling of unfinished business. . . . I felt that it was a challenge and that I would like to see what would happen to it if I gave it a *visual* treatment. . . . My poetry and filmmaking lead individual lives. When I'm not writing, I like the feel of expressing certain things for which there are no words; then I work at the challenges of the nonverbal language of film. So when I feel I have had enough of words, it's nice to be able to turn to filmic expression. Sometimes there's an obsessive need to go and create a vision. I don't say that this vision is always satisfactory for me, but then, this is part of the quest.[28]

The older avant-gardists all became involved in making films for aesthetic reasons which clearly had nothing to do with feminism. Five of the seven made their first films before the spread of the feminist movement (one each in 1963, '64, '66, '67, and '68); though the other two began later (one in 1971, one in 1972), their motives also derived from their aesthetic interests. Nonetheless, they and their films have been claimed by the feminist film movement. Feminist art and film-related journals include articles on the avant-garde filmmakers, and their films are shown at women's film festivals and in women's studies courses. Labelled as "feminist filmmakers" by critics and audiences, the avant-gardists have had to confront a public/political definition at odds with the underlying features of their self-definition as "artists." The ambiguities and contradictions inherent in this role are revealed clearly in the remarks of Amy Greenfield:

> I've never thought of myself as a feminist filmmaker. I thought of myself as a filmmaker. I'm very happy that those festivals are there because women do need it. . . . If I felt within myself that that was the only value of my films, then I wouldn't feel good about it *at all*. But because I've gotten so much support from male filmmakers in the beginning and my films were shown at Millenium before. . . .[29]

Millenium is a general, not feminist, film showcase in New York, and as Greenfield's voice trails off she is implying that her success in the larger, non-feminist world of independent, avant-garde films is very important to her identity as a filmmaker.

The time at which women became filmmakers as well as their standing in the larger avant-garde film world decisively marks their relationship to feminism, and to the feminist film movement. The few filmmakers who began in the mid-sixties and who had established notable professional reputations before the rise of feminism have remained the most distant from and critical of the women's movement; but in spite of their own attitudes, these women are very successful within the feminist film movement. Their prior critical success as avant-garde filmmakers gained them attention within the feminist film world, and their focus on the subjective side of women's experience secured their success.

Gunvor Nelson, a painter turned filmmaker, whose first film (*Schmeerguntz,* 1965–66) won a number of prizes and helped quickly to establish her reputation as an important avant-garde filmmaker, realized that the women's movement was not as essential to her success as to that of other women. When questioned about whether the women's movement had helped create an audience for her films she said: "Yes, there is a certain audience that is created through it, but I wasn't in need as much as some of the other people of an audience."[30]

Avant-garde filmmakers, like many artists, resist sociological, collectivist explanations of and responses to their lives and their work in favor of more personal, individualistic analyses. When Gunvor Nelson spoke of her own life in connection to feminism, for example, she said: "The basic parts of the women's movement is sort of my life. To be independent and believe in oneself."[31]

Storm de Hirsch carried this a step further by proposing an androgenous model of creativity and thus emphasizing *individual* over group (sex-linked) differences:

> *Storm de Hirsch:* I think it's questionable as to whether the biological structure (i.e. sex differences) makes that much difference in terms of art. I feel that when it comes to art, there's a question of soul, of the inner world, that's a universal thing; and I feel that the soul is neither male nor female. When I work and get involved with filmmaking, especially in my animation, I become both man and woman or either one.[32]

Gunvor Nelson, characteristically, also repudiated women's collective efforts to confront their problems as *women* filmmakers:

> . . . there's too much reinforcement of separatism that I don't like. You know, women's film festivals, ... I don't think I would be that different in my difficulties if I were a man.[33]

The three older avant-gardists who are members of a women's film distribution group (Women/Artists/Filmmakers, all members of which are artists and filmmakers) express more positive, unambiguous views of the women's movement. Like the women avant-gardists quoted above, these three have also been claimed by the feminist film movement. But they differ from the women above in that they, in turn, "claim" the women's movement. Their identification with the women's movement predated their collective efforts at film distribution which, in turn, reinforced these women's commitment to and involvement with the feminist film movement. Rosalind Schneider spoke of how important the women's audience has been for her work; the public premiere of her films occurred at the First International Festival of Women's Films in 1972. That screening established her reputation as a woman filmmaker, and her films have been shown at a large number of women's programs and festivals since then.

Rosalind Schneider, a founding member of Women/Artists/Filmmakers (the leading avant-garde film distribution cooperative) criticized the tendency to equate "feminist art" with that which is explicitly political. She recognized that this realistic, didactic conception of feminist art had grown up quickly, and hoped that it would soon make way for a more eclectic, inclusive view in which abstract films would be judged in general, rather than female or feminist, terms. In the first excerpt below, Schneider hints at the subtle relationship which she sees between her own films and feminism. In the second, she equates "individual expression" with feminism.

JR: Do you think of your films as feminist?

Schneider: I have a different definition of what feminist is anyhow. I feel that they're very strongly feminist in one viewpoint and that is I deal with things as a woman would see them.[34]

If we're to accept women as individuals we also have to accept the fact that we all don't think the same way and that we all don't make political statements. . . . By the very nature of making art, that is in itself a political statement.[35]

Male-female differences (social and/or political and/or aesthetic) are the bedrock on which the feminist film movement rests. An important segment of women avant-garde filmmakers (mainly those whose film success preceded the women's movement) do not acknowledge the significance of these differences and thereby undermine the legitimacy of the entire feminist film enterprise. By contrast, avant-gardists whose filmmaking careers are more closely interwoven with the feminist movement are less likely to be critical of its assumptions and activities, and several of them have joined together in a cooperative film distribution project which clearly incorporates feminist principles.

The older documentary filmmakers and the avant-garde filmmakers, both of whom began making films in the early and mid-1960s, followed career paths which differed substantially. Whereas the documentarists typically started out wanting to "make movies," the avant-gardists initially defined themselves as "artists" and eventually extended their early art interests to include film. The older documentary filmmakers have substantially redefined themselves and their work in conjunction with feminism and the feminist film movement: they have come to see themselves as "feminist filmmakers." The avant-gardists have a more tenuous and ambiguous relationship to the feminist film movement. They continue to make films which explore personal consciousness, sexuality, childhood and other ideas compatible with feminism from a more subjective and psychological perspective than the documentarists'. There is much more continuity in the themes of avant-garde films made by women whose primary orientation is toward the world of avant-garde film and art rather than political feminism.

Younger Filmmakers: Documentarists and Avant-Gardists

Younger filmmakers, whether documentarist or avant-gardist, were influenced by the feminist movement from the outset. These women had not established their identities or careers as filmmakers in the pre-feminist past; they came of professional age as the occupation of feminist filmmaker was being created. Some of them, in fact, unknowingly helped create it.

Most of the younger filmmakers interviewed spoke of their entry into filmmaking primarily in terms of feminist "consciousness raising," "education," and "communication." This contrasts with the older filmmakers' desires to "make movies" or to expand their aesthetic boundaries. Most of the younger filmmakers also had long-standing interests and some training in the arts. But faced with the opportunities to create an art that voiced their political views, they willingly committed their art to the service of their feminism.

All of the intentionally feminist filmmakers had been in women's consciousness-raising groups and had turned to filmmaking out of frustration at the endless talk and introspection to which the consciousness-raising process so often led. The following comments offer insights into the reasons why feminists transposed their ideology into film:

> *Julia Reichert:*   After nearly six months of being a five-woman island we began to grow—first to ten, then to many. Eventually I found myself in the leadership position of a very large group of student and non-student women. I wanted to do some sort of project in media about women. . . .[36]

While in college, Reichert previously had done documentary photography, and then studied filmmaking because she "came to realize the limitations of still photography as a medium for conveying social criticism and moving people toward personal and political change."[37] Film seemed to Reichert, as to a number of other filmmakers, to be an obvious way to extend her conjoined interests in politics and the arts. She and her male partner, Jim Klein, made an early feminist film about socialization.

> *Growing Up Female* was the result. We made it to bring about some of the new awareness about women's oppression to a broad audience. We specifically wanted to reach beyond the women's movement to housewives, poor women, black women, high school kids, etc.

Making the interconnections between her feminism and her films even more explicit, Reichert wrote, "I cannot separate my being a filmmaker from being part of the women's movement. And I cannot separate any of that from being part of the movement for Socialism." When she wrote the above, Reichert had melded her New Left orientation apparent in *Growing Up Female* with the growing socialist feminist wing of the women's movement. In 1973 she was a leader of the New American Movement, one of the organizational remnants of the New Left in the 1970s.

Judy Smith, a Newsreel member, also described the way in which she and other women at San Francisco Newsreel saw themselves in relation to filmmaking, feminism, and New Left politics in 1970. Smith regarded her feminist film project as thoroughly political, as did other Newsreel members, and even approached formal and stylistic problems from a consciously political perspective.

Smith: And we really felt that with *The Woman's Film* we were somehow going to define a new type of Newsreel film. That it wasn't going to be garbled; it wasn't going to be pictures you couldn't see. There were going to be clear images. We wanted it to be suitable for television, suitable for mass production [she means distribution]. That we could make a lot of money on. And that people could see as a real movie instead of sort of a scratched image.

JR: Did you see that as a compromise?

Smith: No, it was seen as coming from a political base which means that we really wanted to reach masses of people, instead of just students and hippies. The group was defining itself more and more in terms of workers. Being Marxist-Leninists, reaching the proletariat. And *The Woman's Film* was going to define our politics in terms of that.[38]

The earliest explicitly feminist films were about social issues which directly incorporated contemporary liberationist thinking. In making films about feminist issues, these filmmakers were trying to "spread the word," to extend the reach of their own newly developed understanding. They did not see themselves as the source, the ideological innovators, of feminist thinking, but rather as its communicators, paralleling the role which their New Left predecessor, Newsreel, defined for itself vis-à-vis the radical movement of the 60s. (See Bill Nichols, 1972, for a fuller discussion of the relationship between Newsreel and the New Left.) In playing out this mediating role, the feminist film movement changed in concert with the larger feminist movement and the related societal changes of the 1970s.

The majority of younger women began making films in order to communicate their feminist politics. Only later, as they became more involved in feminist film activities (festivals, distribution groups) and came to be regarded as filmmakers by others, did they define themselves as much by their filmmaker roles as by their feminism. One filmmaker who began as an editor put it succinctly when she said, "I never even thought of myself as a filmmaker until other people started calling me one."[39] Magazine articles which featured the women and their films, film festivals which showed their work, distribution cooperatives, and related events all gave these women visibility as *feminist filmmakers*. Women who had started out to make one feminist film began another, and their careers were underway.

A number of feminist filmmakers began by making documentaries about feminist social and political issues, but many of them have moved to less polemical, more introspective films which explore individual women's lives more fully. This tendency reflects the documentary filmmakers' changing motives and ideology and brings them closer to the interests of avant-garde filmmakers. In discussing the biographical and autobiographical portrait films, the documentary filmmakers revealed a heightened interest in personal experience and the familial context in which it is embedded. Several of them explicitly linked this to role changes and life cycle transitions they were undergoing or anticipated undergoing. Both Amalie Rothschild (in *Nana, Mom, and Me,* 1974) and Joyce Chopra (*Joyce at 34,* 1972, a forerunner of this subgenre) make it clear that becoming a mother, or the anticipation of that change, sparked their interest in filming their own mothers and grandmothers. *Joyce at 34* took form during Chopra's pregnancy and developed in conversations Joyce Chopra had with a friend, a woman sociologist, about "the changes in a woman's relationship with her mother when the woman becomes a mother."[40]

Nana, Mom, and Me, for example, opens with a full shot of Amalie Rothschild, at once a filmmaker and film subject, who says directly to the audience:

> When you start thinking of yourself as a mother, you have to stop thinking of yourself as a child. I see my parents in a new way. I've begun to feel the continuity between generations as well as the change.

Similarly, a life change for Geri Ashur; the loss of her mother, led her in the same personal, biographical direction. Ashur's recent film portrait, *Libba Cotten* (1976), expresses feelings about motherhood and generational continuity that were catalyzed by her mother's death. Ashur described the appeal of her heroine Libba Cotten in the following way:

> . . . She had this large family. She only had one daughter, but the daughter had five, and those five had more. So its like generations and generations of Cottens. Thats what attracted me. My mother had also died, so there was something about the total maternality [sic] that she represents. A lot of the film is actually her talking about her mother.[41]

Many of the portrait filmmakers now feel that they have reached the end of the possibilities which this type of film offers. They hope to make larger feature films which allow them to communicate their feminist values and insights to large audiences, while at the same time furthering and expanding their own careers as filmmakers. Most of them have grown restless under the weight of the label, "feminist filmmaker." When this occupational category first emerged, it legitimated their activities and aspirations to themselves and to other feminists and independent filmmakers. But now it has begun to hinder their career advancement by pigeonholing them too narrowly. Well over half of the documentarists (but only a couple of the avant-gardists) are searching for ways to extend their personal feminist interests and insights (about women, relationships between women, and families) into commercially viable feature-length films.

As a means of moving into commercial feature films, a number of the women have taken the tack of writing scripts and film treatments for possible production. They recognized that scriptwriting was a more accessible route to making feature films than directing, where opportunities arc vcry tightly circumscribed. These women made it clear, however, that they see scriptwriting largely as a way station to directing, their long-term goal. As one woman put it, "I really want to direct feature films. . . . If you're a writer you want to write a novel. If you're in film, you want to do a feature."[42]

While scriptwriting is the most likely route, a few have tried alternative paths to the director's chair. Nell Cox fought for and was finally given a $200,000 grant by the Los Angeles public television station to produce a low-budget feature film. Martha Coolidge solicited backers to raise the $65,000 she needed to make her "transition" film, a fictionalized documentary entitled *Not a Pretty Picture*. The viability of these routes, however, is yet to be fully demonstrated.

The careers and interests of the main types of filmmakers, which were briefly synthesized by the energy and support of the feminist movement, are likely to diverge again in the near future. Initially the feminist movement created a new set of career opportunities for creative women, women who had previously been blocked from careers in art. For the realist documentary filmmakers, feminism suggested new themes; and it was in developing these themes, for which there was an increasingly popular demand, that they gained a limited area of mobility in a competitive film world. In the 1970s, as the filmmakers matured and the initial insights they caught in their films were institutionalized, they began to turn inward and refocus their cameras on private themes—family and interpersonal relationships—which now seem increasingly dominant. These themes can more readily be absorbed into ongoing feature film traditions, especially those of the European directors who rose to prominence in America in the 1960s and heavily influenced many of these women during the formative high school and college years. Considered collectively, the documentarists clearly hope some day to produce films within the traditions developed by the European masters.

The avant-garde filmmakers, on the other hand, seem more likely to continue in the tradition of personal expression in which they are anchored. Relatively unconcerned with political and social issues, they often express the hope that in the upcoming decade they will continue to mature as artists in their current genre while achieving sufficient success to relieve themselves of their financial worries. Their work, unlike its reception, has not been greatly affected by the feminist movement. Future changes in avant-garde films by both men and women are likely to emerge from sources internal to the art/film world rather than from social or political transformations in the larger society.

Although their career paths are likely to diverge once again, with documentarists moving into fiction filmmaking, most of the filmmakers discussed here can be expected to continue making films. Their careers and identities as filmmakers are now firmly established, and there is no reason to believe that emerging family commitments will obliterate their filmmaking careers. On the contrary, several feminist filmmakers have already used this career/family conflict as the central problematic in their films. Like so many other working women in the 1960s and 1970s, feminist filmmakers will juggle and meld familial and occupational roles.

4

The Films

Introduction

The major focus of this chapter will be a description and analysis of feminist films. The three primary clusters of feminist films to be discussed are: (1) the social issue documentary films and (2) the personal portrait documentaries, which together lie at the core of the feminist film movement, and (3) the women's avant-garde films, which are at the periphery. These ideal film types are discussed, analyzed, and compared in terms of four major analytic dimensions: (1) social structural vs. individual/personal definitions of women's issues, (2) collectivist vs. individualist responses to women's problems, (3) temporal orientation inherent in each film type, and (4) rational vs. expressive type of understanding which each film type assumes and promotes.

Documentary films about feminist issues (e.g. abortion, women's economic and social status, socialization) were first produced in 1969–70 and screened in 1970–71. They represented the onset of the feminist film movement. These films focused on the gender-linked status and public roles of contemporary women, typically stressing both women's oppression and their ability to fight against such oppression. Issue films reflected the concerns and perspective of the younger branch of the women's movement at the time they were made. Most of the early films were didactic and depicted women's lives from an issue-oriented and social-structural perspective, focusing on shared problems which women face as women. "Women's liberation cinema," in the words of one reviewer writing in 1972, referred to ". . . films made expressly to educate, to raise consciousness, to help create the forces for change."[1] Nine of the 11 films which McCormick discussed in her essay were issue films: they explored topics like abortion, sex-role socialization, and the broader issue of "women's place." (The other two films were portraits.)

In 1974 a second wave of feminist films, biographical and autobiographical portraits, crested. The film portraits reflected feminists' (and others) mounting concerns with private life; they focus in closely on the life and identity of a specific woman. Older female relatives or the filmmaker herself are frequently cast as the central character. Typically the central protagonist is an anonymous woman shown struggling with quintessential female issues, for example, trying to establish and maintain an identity as a worker as well as a wife and mother (*Joyce at 34; Nana, Mom and Me*), combatting sex discrimination (*Antonia*), living a meaningful life as a single woman outside of the nuclear family (*Yudie*). (*Antonia* could be interpreted as a film portrait of Antonia Brico, or as an issue film about sex discrimination. Within this study it is defined as a "mixed" film.) Film portraits reveal connections between public and private aspects of women's lives. Like the women's movement, they identify points at which the personal and political dimensions of women's lives intersect.

Famous women whose lives are extraordinary sometimes "star" in feminist film portraits, e.g. Gertrude Stein, Mary Cassatt, and Louise Nevelson. Unlike the anonymous women commonly featured, these women are depicted in terms that separate them from most other women; their unique, distinctive qualities are emphasized over their typical, representative ones. The film *Antonia,* featuring the now-famous orchestra conductor Antonia Brico, differs from this pattern; *Antonia* emphasizes the stark sex discrimination which plagued this very talented woman. Ironically, the film portrait did more to boost Brico's career than rave reviews of her conducting had done over the years. (A conversation with filmmaker, Jill Godmillow, confirmed my impressions that conducting opportunities had opened considerably for Ms. Brico since the film first appeared.)

Issue and portrait films are made with an eye to the context in which they are viewed. Most often they are shown in educational settings which allow for and presume postfilm discussions. The films are intended to provoke discussions among the viewers which, in turn, generate new feminist insights and commitments.

By contrast, women's avant-garde films reverberate with private expressions of individualist values and themes. Even those films which concern feminist themes (women's sexuality, identity, childhood) approach them in highly individualized and personal, not political, ways. They deal with private moods, feelings, and interior experiences rather than with sequences of action. These three basic types of films developed at different times, and are related to different tendencies within the women's movement. Consequently they express and reveal key tensions within feminism. Both social issue and personal portrait documentaries grew directly out of different stages of the women's movement and clearly reflect different feminist themes, values, and commitments. By contrast, many of the most important women's avant-garde films, now regarded as feminist, predate the women's movement: they have been reinterpreted as feminist and claimed by the feminist film movement.

In describing and analyzing the films, special attention must be given to the larger political context in which the films are produced and viewed. Changes in American culture and in the orientation of the feminist movement provide the background against which changes in the themes and definitions of feminist films are assessed.

In the final section of this chapter each cluster of feminist films is analyzed with primary emphasis on linking the films' themes to issues and tensions in the contemporary feminist movement. Tensions between social structural and individual/personal definitions of women's issues, and between collectivist and individualist responses to women's problems, are central to this analysis. In addition, two important subthemes connect the films to different ideas and tendencies in the feminist movement: the view of time and the relative emphasis on rational or expressive types of understanding further differentiate the three basic film types. Each type of film confers distinct meaning on the past, present, and future. Issue documentaries are present and future oriented, portraits reclaim and integrate the past within a broader feminist temporal perspective, and avant-garde films transcend notions of past, present, and future. As Mannheim pointed out in his studies of social change and social thought, the orientation to time provides important clues to the value orientations of a social movement.[2]

Documentary and avant-garde films also differ significantly in terms of the bases of their appeal. Issue documentaries are the most heavily rationalist in their approach. By presenting authoritative information they attempt to persuade the audience of their position's legitimacy. Film portraits employ both rational and emotional types of understanding; they place special emphasis on the emotional context of social action and elicit the audience's empathy, or *verstehen*, in responding to them.[3] Avant-garde films are the most expressive of the three. They neither present factual information nor depict human experience from a realistic perspective. Avant-garde films convey the filmmaker's emotions and subjective sense of an experience or situation.

The Larger Political Context

Changes in the larger political context of American society and in the feminist movement from 1966 through 1976 set the stage for understanding changes in the themes and definitions of feminist films. The current

American political climate contrasts sharply with that of the sixties; between 1966 and 1977 there was a marked decline in left-liberal public political activity. Though commentators may argue about the meaning of this reorientation of American culture, none doubt that it has occurred. The conventional wisdom is quite pessimistic. Christopher Lasch, Tom Wolfe, and others argue that Americans are becoming ensnared in ruthlessly individualistic narcissism. The seemingly endless appeal of various self-help movements (EST, assertiveness training, Esalen) and best-selling books on how to say no without guilt, how to be your own best friend, and how to get power and use it are taken as conclusive evidence that Americans have retreated from politics and have become obsessed with gratifying their personal appetites for money, power, and sex.[4] One recent analyst wrote:

> If the sixties can be tagged as a decade of politics, then the tag for the seventies is personal. In the sixties, personal fulfillment seemed a self-indulgent bourgeois luxury; in the seventies, politics appears to many as ineffectual, unfeeling, even anti-social.[5]

Parallel shifts characterize the women's movement during the same period. Many commentators have glibly assumed that privatization signifies a repudiation of core feminist values and hence the demise of the contemporary women's movement. The death of the women's movement has been trumpeted repeatedly during the last three years; the requiem is becoming a recurring chorus. According to one prominent feminist:

> From all sides, now, they are tolling the bell to mourn the death of the women's movement in America. . . .
>
> The newspapers—and even the women's movement's own press—began to headline "Does the Women's Movement Still Have Clout?" "Is NOW on the Brink of Then?"[6]

Privatization of the women's movement parallels, but is distinct from, the narcissism mentioned above. Privatization indicates that some feminists are involved in the difficult and demanding task of integrating feminist values into their personal lives, rather than rejecting such values. It should be reemphasized that the radical feminist component of the contemporary feminist movement has emphasized the personal dimensions of feminist values from the outset. In part, the unification of the women's movement around 1972 signalled a broader consensus among feminists on what was initially a radical feminist position—the political/theoretical importance of private experience for feminist politics. The infusion of younger women into the mainstream of the women's movement, coupled with exposure to more radical theories analyzing the position of women in American society, radicalized somewhat the goals and tactics of the former rights branch.[7]

In addition to the diffusion of political ideas from one sector of the women's movement to the others, it seems likely that women were following the same internal dialectic which characterized earlier generations of feminist activists.[8] Women whose initial interests in feminism were structural and collectivist—directed at collectively reforming or transforming social institutions which discriminated against women—redirected their energies from the public sphere to the private one and attempted to reform or transform their personal social relationships.

Rossi has argued that social change involves a predictable dialectic between the public and private expression of core values. Individuals (or generations) who engage in highly visible public activity in the political arena in one stage of their lives may struggle to apply the same values to the personal, private sphere in the next stage (or the next generation). Each stage strengthens the entire fabric of social change: public, political behavior has an impact on social institutions and private behavior has an impact on personal life. Through this dialectic public ideas are translated into the stuff of private lives.

Feminists' autobiographical accounts document and help illuminate the privatization of the women's movement. Betty Friedan now speaks about the importance of redefining traditional female tasks like cooking from a feminist perspective. She concluded her article on cooking by stating:

> We women had to liberate ourselves from the slavish necessities, the excessive drudgery and guilt related to cooking in order to be able to now liberate ourselves from an excessive need to react against it. As for me I've come out the other end of women's liberation to make my own soup.[9]

It is clear that Friedan has not retreated from feminist values, but is incorporating them in her life on a different, more personal level. In a similar vein, a recent anthology on "women and work" emphasizes the personal dimensions of this standard feminist issue. *Working It Out* presents autobiographical accounts of individual women's formative experiences regarding work and the problems in developing a career as a feminist.[10] There seems to be a shift from statistical evidence of occupational discrimination, which kept women on the "outside," characteristic of the early 1970s, to concern for coping strategies, with how to survive and grow as a feminist "inside" the mainstream occupational system.

Conclusive statements about the dialectic between feminists' public political activity and the private consolidation of feminist values demand considerably more research than yet exists, but a good deal of evidence from feminist filmmakers and films supports this more optimistic, dialectical interpretation of the privatization depicted in the films. (See chapter 3 for a fuller discussion of this.)

Population and Sample

As seen in chapter 3, feminist filmmaking is primarily a product of the 1970s. Although it began later than other feminist art and media, it has grown rapidly. By the end of 1976 about 250 feminist films had been produced. There is no complete listing of feminist films, or even total agreement on the term "feminist film," so it is not possible to define the population exactly. Films widely designated as feminist are directed by women; their content concerns women's issues and/or lives, or, in the case of avant-garde films, their content expresses women's sensibility. The population size given here is estimated on the basis of listings in major directories, entries in women's festivals, film screenings, and information acquired informally within the women's film movement.[11]

The sample of films discussed in this chapter includes all of the feminist films made by the 30 sample filmmakers. Their non-feminist films are not included in this investigation. Sample films are classified as "issue," "portrait," or "avant-garde." The distinction between issue and portrait documentaries, on the one hand, and avant-garde films on the other are readily apparent, even to a novice. Distinctions between issue and portrait documentaries, however, are not so clear and obvious. Many feminist documentaries actually combine elements of these two analytically distinct types. Anticipating the problem of film classification, I approached and secured the cooperation of two core members of the feminist film movement, to assist me in the task of classification. Both of the other women had served on more than three major festival screening committees and had written articles on feminist films. The raters first differentiated documentaries from avant-garde films, and then classified each sample documentary as predominantly an issue film, a portrait film, or a mixed film that equally combined elements of both ideal types. Agreement between two raters was deemed sufficient to classify a film. Table 2 presents a classification of the sample films, by film type and year of release. (See below.)

It is interesting to note that many films made before 1970 which were neither intended as feminist statements nor initially viewed in those terms by critics or audiences have been relabelled and incorporated into the repertory of feminist films. These "proto-feminist" films, produced be-

Table 2.   Sample Films, by Type and Date of Release

Type of Film	Year of Release								
	pre-69	69	70	71	72	73	74	75	76	Total
Issue	0	2	1	7	1	1	1	4	2	19
Portrait	0	2	1	0	2	2	3	0	5	15
Mixed	0	0	1	3	2	2	1	1	0	10
Avant-Garde	3	4	2	7	8	3	1	0	3	31
Total	3	8	5	17	13	8	6	5	10	75

tween 1966 and 1972, foreshadowed many themes and styles of the feminist film movement. Several examples will illustrate the ways in which films have been redefined as feminist.

I Am Somebody is a documentary film about black women hospital workers who strike for better pay and job conditions. Although it was produced as a pro-union and civil rights film, it has become a feminist film "classic." It is mentioned in the three main printed guides to the feminist film movement and is widely known among film movement members. The filmmaker (a black woman) included themes of sexist discrimination alongside those of racism and anti-unionism. She even touched on some personal ramifications of women's political activism. A strike leader's husband, forced to take on her housework and child care tasks, gains some insight into the double day which she (and most employed women) typically work. Like its themes, its style anticipates later developments in feminist documentaries. First, the film consists primarily of unstaged footage, thus underscoring the significance of ordinary women's experience. In addition, the film's narrator is a woman worker who became a prominent strike leader. During the course of the strike she was transformed from a quiet, apolitical worker into an effective spokeswoman and leader who maintains a strong commitment to her husband and children. A tape of her reminiscences about the meaning of the strike provides the concluding narration for the film.

I Am Somebody is consistent with a range of feminist values and interests, e.g. problems of poor women, black women, of juggling family, career, and political activism, and of sexual politics (of housework or child care) within marriage. Because of its showing at the First International Festival of Women's Films *I Am Somebody* became identified as a feminist film. It now plays regularly to two distinct audiences: feminists and unionists.[12] Its continued success is based heavily on the fact that it integrates political and personal dimensions of women's lives. In addition, it is one of the only films made by a black woman about black women.[13]

Diane (1969) was also redefined and claimed as a feminist film although it was not originally intended or received as such. This film portrait of a troubled mid-Western woman, an aspiring actress adrift in New York City, was made before the filmmaker knew of the women's movement. It explores the conflicts which tug at the protagonist, but the film never connects Diane's personal problems (with men, with her career) to the general problems which confront women as a group. It does not, in other words, present a feminist structural analysis. Within the context of feminism, however, *Diane* is often viewed as typifying the pitfalls which beset women in their quintessentially female roles as models and actresses. Like *I Am Somebody,* when *Diane* was shown at the first Festival of Women's Films its reputation as a feminist film was established. Since then it has been shown in two major women's film festivals and is featured in one of the printed guides to the movement. It is distributed by an alternative distribution company, and listed in their "Women's Films" section.

Among proto-feminist avant-garde films, none anticipates feminist themes, images, and sensibilities more closely than *Schmeerguntz*. Made in 1965–66 by two women, *Schmeerguntz* is a collage of contradictory images of pregnancy, childbirth, and childrearing. It juxtaposes idealized photographs of brides and children with vivid images of toilets filled with excrement, of dirty diapers, of babies eating and throwing up. Visually and thematically, *Schmeerguntz* immerses a viewer in the "shit work" of domesticity. It was made well before the rise of the women's movement, and emerged directly from the immediacy of the filmmakers' personal experiences. When they made *Schmeerguntz,* both filmmakers were wives and mothers of young children, and one of them was pregnant. *Schmeerguntz* was an instant success within the avant-garde, and was shown in the First International Festival of Women's Films in 1972. As with the other proto-feminist films, this marked the beginning of its new reputation as a feminist film.

Abstract films which depict sexuality have also been adopted by the feminist film movement. Connie Beeson's sentimentalized films are listed in all three printed guides, and they were shown in three of the four sample festivals. Beeson made *Unfolding,* her film of a man and woman making love, in 1969, clearly before the rise of the feminist film movement. She did not intend her film as a "feminist statement" but acknowledged that it has been much more widely shown since the rise of the women's movement.[14]

Thus, the feminist film movement has claimed films which pre-date it but whose themes anticipate feminist ones; additional attempts were made to claim films by women whose artistic reputations were already well established. The burgeoning feminist film movement tried to claim Shirley Clarke, a renowned cinéma vérité filmmaker, because of her reputation as a leading independent filmmaker, not for the themes of her films. Clarke actively resisted being incorporated in, or claimed by, the feminist film movement. She refused to allow her films to be screened at the First International Festival of Women's Films. According to the Festival organizer, Clarke was initially ambivalent but leaning toward consent, about being included in a women's film festival. But in the end, she withdrew her film and severed her connections with the Women's Festival. The Festival organizer said, "At first she said I could show *Portrait of Jason* and it came to May . . . and Shirley Clarke said *she didn't want to be known as a women's filmmaker*."[15] Shirley Clarke has not cooperated with most feminist film programs or projects since that time, rejecting identification as a "women's filmmaker." Other filmmakers have objected to being considered only a feminist filmmaker, but none of them have gone as far as Clarke and actually refused to allow their films to be shown in feminist programs or festivals.

Feminist Films; Issue, Portrait, and Avant-Garde

This section details the concerns, contours, and meanings of feminist films—social issue films, personal portrait documentaries, and avant-garde films. It explores the relationship between each film type and different tendencies in the feminist movement.

Issue Films

Issue films approach the experiences of life, work, politics, sexuality, and the events of daily life from a social structural perspective. The themes of issue films delineate the shared, socially structured limitations, oppression, and discrimination which women suffer as a group. Taken together, they focus on a range of problems central to women's lives and to the women's movement, e.g. abortion, day care, sexuality, and work. *Growing Up Female; As Six Become One*, for example, surveys the inculcation of traditional female roles and attitudes in women and young girls and points accusingly at the schools, advertising media, and parents for molding young girls to the narrow groove of traditional roles and options.

In issue films the women typically differ in age, social class, race, and personal style; this device subtly suggests a comprehensive, broad unity in all women's experiences despite their diversity of social characteristics. What may look like an individual experience at the beginning of the film, especially to an uninitiated audience, looks like a concrete manifestation of a general social problem by the end. The recordings of such experiences are compressed cinematic simulations of the consciousness-raising process; they convey the sense of a common and therefore social problem, a sense that develops when a number of individuals reveal to the group problems which they had considered unique and private.

Early issue documentaries resemble consciousness raising in structure as well as intention. Women speak in their own words about various problematic aspects of their lives. Their dawning feminist awareness is simulated on screen; a woman is typically shown talking first to herself, and then to a small group of other women who are, or represent, a consciousness-raising group. These films provide a plausible context for explicitly discussing one's life within a feminist perspective.

Different cinematic techniques express the structural emphasis of issue films. Most films stylistically reinforce their themes by intercutting interviews with a number of rather diverse women whose experiences are strikingly similar. Their lives and analyses overlap and build on each other. As the women talk to the camera and to each other, their parallel narratives are intercut and lead to similar conclusions. A unified, coherent description emerges. Each woman's story then lends credibility and legitimacy to the others and to the emerging totality.

The Woman's Film (1971) and *Woman to Woman* (1975) are typical issue films which portray women's lives from a structural perspective. Like many of the liberationist analyses published in 1971–72 (e.g. *Sexual Politics, Woman's Estate*), they do not focus on a single issue but provide a comprehensive analysis of women's lives and status. By contrasting common features from many diverse women's lives, they piece together a picture of the subordination and degradation inherent in a "woman's place."

The form of *The Woman's Film* emphasizes the connections between the personal and the political. The film opens with a rhythmic collage of still photographs which cut from those showing mythologized views of women (mostly advertising photos of brides and fashion models) to those showing ordinary, even haggard, women doing routine work. A number of photos are of women's hands, busy at domestic work, washing dishes, dusting, or diapering a baby. The brief opening collage sequence is followed by a sequence of long narratives by several women who talk directly to the audience about their own hopes, experiences, and consciousness of their roles as women. Each of these women was filmed in her home where she is shown in close-up as she recounts her life story. The shared fantasies about marriage, the common problems of poor and working-class women weave themselves together into a tapestry of women's oppression. One woman talks of her impoverished childhood.

Epitomizing her deprivation, she confides that there wasn't even enough money for candy or soda pop. She tells of trying to escape her childhood through marriage, and of her inevitable disappointment, all of which paved the way to her eventual feminist consciousness. Another woman explains that her former husband devised a detection scheme to make sure that she didn't leave the house when he was at work. A third rhythmically intones about the endless chores which she did, first as her father's daughter, and then as her husband's wife. She, too, had erroneously thought that marriage meant an escape from the drudgery of her early life.

As these incidents indicate, all of the central issues and characters in *The Woman's Film* suggest that the women's movement has a working-class social base and political orientation. Its New Left filmmakers, three women in the San Francisco Newsreel group, substituted their conception of what they felt the women's movement ought to be for what it was (and still is, to a large extent)—a predominantly middle-class movement.

The filmed narratives are all spoken to the audience in quiet voices, almost monotones. As the women speak, the camera remains focused on them in close-up and medium shots. The power of these autobiographical sequences derives from the stories they tell and is enhanced by the contrast between the dramatic, poignant events the women describe and the understated way in which they relate them.[16]

This sequence of individual women's stories is followed by a montage of drawings of slaves coupled with Oscar Brown Jr.'s moving slave auction song, "Bid 'Em In." The juxtaposition of the slavery sequence with the preceding one of contemporary women suggests an analogy between the positions of the two groups. This analogy was extensively used in the women's movement when *The Woman's Film* was being made (1969–71) but has been sharply criticized since then, mainly by black women. In the next section of *The Woman's Film,* groups of women are shown talking together in consciousness-raising sessions. As in parts of the women's movement, consciousness raising is the process by which women become more aware of their situation as women and gain the confidence to do something about it. In *The Woman's Film* individual awareness grows out of the consciousness-raising process and leads to collective action directed at social problems.

The final emphasis of *The Woman's Film* is on women's political action. Those who have talked about their lives from the privacy of their homes in earlier segments are shown outside in their public roles as strikers and demonstrators. Vanda, once a captive wife, is shown with other women as they collectively picket while their husbands strike.

Woman to Woman (1975) is a broad cinematic survey of women's lives and women's work. It covers women's historical and contemporary work experience and status—the former through old movie footage and the latter through interviews with contemporary women of various ages, personal (life style and sexual) orientations, ethnic and racial backgrounds, and social classes.

> The film opens with an historical sequence using stock footage, still photographs, and music to trace the changes, decade by decade, in women's roles (work roles in particular). It argues that women's work, and the respect or lack of it, in which it is held, is a function of the state of society and of the economy at any given point in our history. Contemporary women are interviewed in a variety of surroundings; a nude dancer in her dressing room, housewives around a kitchen table, inmates of the women's jail in San Francisco, an ex-prostitute organizing a movement to have prostitution decriminalized. The point is made that much of women's work has never been considered to be of sufficient difficulty or economic value to be dignified with the appelation "work." Women of widely varying occupations suffer from many of the same disadvantages and experience similar problems.[17]

In grounding its views of women's roles in a wide range of real women's lives and experiences, *Woman to Woman* displays its structural approach to reality. As in *The Woman's Film,* the significance of each individual vignette is established by those which surround it. The common ideological and social structures in which women's lives are embedded, rather than any individual life, unify the film.

　　Taking Our Bodies Back (1974) and *Becoming Tough Enough* (1975) are characteristic of more recently produced feminist issue films; both delineate specific contemporary issues—women's health and assertiveness—through interviews with a wide range of women. *Taking Our Bodies Back* documents the expanding women's health movement; it highlights medical problems which women face, such as hysterectomies, abortions, and breast cancer, while presenting women's collective responses to these problems, e.g. self-help clinics and home births. The filmmakers' description conveys the film's political perspective and contents.

> This film documents a growing movement of women to regain control of their bodies. It shows women learning about their bodies, and teaching other women. It shows women becoming aware of their rights in dealing with medicine, an industry which can no longer expect women to be grateful, passive and ignorant.[18]

Taking Our Bodies Back has social structural and collectivist perspectives. First, the film is edited so that many women's experiences and observations overlap to suggest a widely shared, socially structured problem. Next, it documents and endorses the collective political basis of the women's health movement by showing how groups of women have collectively developed alternatives to the traditional delivery of women's health care.

Finally, it was made and distributed by three people who, in accord with their commitment to collectivist work processes and values, do not even identify themselves by name in the film or in the catalogue. This is the only example of self-imposed anonymity I have encountered in feminist films. Although the tensions between commitment to collectivist values and aspirations toward individual success continue to tug feminists in opposing directions, all other filmmakers have publicly laid claim to their work by signing it.

The feminists' emphasis on collectivism represents a profound counterpoint to women's traditional isolation. The women's movement has made significant inroads into the sense of what is "private" by pointing out the ways in which women's isolation in the home reinforces traditional female powerlessness and subordination. In feminist documentary films themselves, and in the discussions which often follow the showing, a privileged place is given to de-privatizing those experiences and feelings once regarded as strictly personal. Audience discussion after the showing of such a film often entails the same consciousness-raising process depicted in the film itself. Issue and many portrait films are supposed to help stir audience members to a higher level of awareness of their own lives and of the sexist institutions within which those lives are enmeshed and molded. They are intended to simulate and stimulate consciousness-raising discussions, to educate viewers, and within the most political films, to prod them toward feminist political action. In discussing the functions of feminist films, one filmmaker emphasized their educational and political implications.

> Films can tend to promote an understanding and a sense of collective struggle among different sectors of the population. . . . Films can also suggest new political ideas and raise the level of struggle within the movement. *The Woman's Film,* for example, raises issues broader than just feminist issues, like the issue of class struggle.[19]

Social movements vary in their conceptions of past, present, and future. The meaning, depiction, and evaluation of time provide an important clue to the value orientations of social movements, as Karl Mannheim demonstrated in his classic studies.[20] Liberal and radical social movements may anticipate the dawning of a new era in the future, or they may nostalgically hark back to some golden age. Sometimes they combine both temporal orientations. By contrast, conservative social movements typically root value and meaning in the past. In contrasting three major historical forms of utopian mentalities, liberalism, conservatism, and Chiliasm, Mannheim relied heavily on their respective conceptions of past, present, and future.

Whereas for liberalism the future was everything and the past nothing, the conservative mode of experiencing time found the best corroboration of its sense of determinateness in discovering the significance of the past, in the discovery of time as the creator of value. Duration did not exist at all for the Chiliastic mentality, and existed for liberalism only in so far as henceforth it gives birth to progress.[21]

Feminist films can also be analyzed in terms of their depiction and evaluation of past, present, and future. In issue films women talk about their pasts from the viewpoint of the "enlightened present." Time is divided between the false consciousness of the past and the heightened consciousness of the present. Women discuss their pasts in negative terms to illustrate the kinds of culturally induced blindness, degradation, and discrimination which they used to suffer. The films' styles, as well as their themes, derive in part from this bifurcated view of time. Typically the protagonists are visualized in the present. As they discuss their lives we see them in close-up, talking directly to the camera, and in medium shots frequently doing household chores. The past is not visually depicted in the films in which it is repudiated. Issue films present a tightly circumscribed view of the past by limiting the audience's vision to the contemporary viewpoint of the protagonist. There are several reasons for this. First, significant others such as a spouse, parent, or friend from the subject's former relationships are often described in uncomplimentary ways in the films. It is not likely that these people would willingly play out the oppressive roles into which they are being cast. This is clear, for example, in *The Woman's Film,* where the key women critically discuss their former husbands; in *Woman to Woman* where they lambast their former husbands, employers, and psychiatrists; and in many other issue films. Even if the people were willing to appear in the film, they are often quite far from the location where the film is being shot. In films made on very small budgets, it is simply not economically feasible to reassemble such people. In *The Birth Film*, a documentary on a family's experiences with a home birth, there are no direct references to a bleak, oppressive past, but the film conveys a strong sense of new beginnings in an enlightened present. The principal characters (and the filmmaker) view home births as if they were a modern innovation.

Rather than claiming home births as a contemporary feminist invention, the film might have dissected this current trend from historical or cross-cultural perspectives. A good deal of feminist literature on home births does make these connections: the language and conceptual framework for this perspective are definitely available. But *The Birth Film* exhibits a present mindedness characteristic of its time and its genre.

Janie's Janie, a "mixed" film which combines issue and portrait traits, explicitly presents a bleak view of women's past as seen through the prism of the protagonist's present life. We see the narrator as she talks about her life history; her words, emphases, and expressions are our handle on her past. The audience is not permitted to actually view scenes from the past (through old photos or film footage) or to hear about it from other people's perspectives. This ties us all the more firmly to the narrator's view of that which she is describing.

Finally, the three major types of feminist films base their appeal on diverse and disparate values and types of understanding. All three film types evoke elements of expressive and rational understanding, but the balance between these differs significantly in issue, portrait, and avant-garde films. Rational understanding denotes a clear, intellectual (logical or mathematical) grasp of an issue or idea. To the extent that they transmit factual information, issue films are the most heavily rationalist in their approach. But even in issue films, the dramatic presentation of the information, as opposed to a precise, logical formulation, involves an expressive/aesthetic approach.

Issue films project the observable behavior of a number of subjects who are assumed to "represent" the larger population under consideration. In one typical case, a film on abortion (*It Happens to Us,* 1971) juxtaposes a sequence of interviews with women who have had abortions with statistical data about the incidence of abortion and a factual narrative about the medical dangers it entails. While the interviews in the issue films often reveal very personal and passionate responses, underneath them runs a rationalist philosophy: factual knowledge of the issue is expected to educate the film audiences and to persuade them of the validity of a feminist perspective on women's lives.[22]

Portrait Films

Eight film portraits of and by women premiered in 1974. They were widely screened for women's groups and at women's film programs, and two of them were shown at the very prestigious New York Film Festival. Portrait films were widely reviewed in various feminist journals and featured prominently in women's film festivals. Film portraits quickly captured feminists' collective attention and imagination.

Portrait films center around an individual woman, typically one whose life crystallizes and dramatizes significant features of women's roles. In contrast to the overtly collectivist themes and structures of most issue films, the focus in film portraits is not explicitly on feminist issues, but on a specific older woman whose life history gives shape to the film, and whose character is held up as a model for the audience. These women typically demonstrate the considerable spunk which allowed them to

overcome major obstacles in their lives. Many film portraits depict someone whose changing status has made her highly conscious of and well
able to articulate her problematic identity. There are biographies of older
relatives (*Yudie*, 1974; *Old Fashioned Woman,* 1974), autobiographical
films about the filmmaker herself (*Joyce at 34,* 1972; *Nana, Mom, and
Me,* 1974; *Living With Peter,* 1972), and films about women who are not
part of the filmmakers' families (*Not Together Now: End of a Marriage,*
1976; *Woo Who May Wilson,* 1969; *Diane,* 1969; *Libba Cotten,* 1976).

Portrait films reflect feminists' mounting concerns with private life
and often depict women trying to integrate feminist values into their personal lives. The history of a well-known portrait film, *Yudie,* crystallizes
these alternating feminist (political and personal) impulses and provides
a good illustration of Rossi's notion of the public/private dialectic. The
filmmaker, Mirra Bank, spoke freely of how her film changed from an
explicitly political statement (her original conception when she began the
film in 1972) to a more personal one during the two and a half years in
which she shot and edited it.

> *Filmmaker:* I was very involved in the women's movement. . . . I started making
> *Yudie* for that reason. I wanted to make this very pro-woman film, at that time what
> I would call a feminist film, about a woman who had always taken care of herself,
> who lived alone. . . . And I wanted her to put down marriage and put down everything
> (everything connected to women's traditional roles) but she was much more interest-
> ing, much too strong a personality for me to impose that on her. And one of the
> blessings in the fact that it took so long to make the film is that I was forced to grow
> with it and to go deeper and learn more and get a richer thing than had I been able
> to do what I was originally trying to do.[23]

Portrait films about women's personal lives and interpersonal relationships, while often motivated by feminist values, tap two opposing
impulses and are open to contradictory interpretations. They express feminist social values transposed to personal life at the same time that they
express narcissistic, inward-looking yearnings within the dominant culture. Audience members may bring their own perspectives to the films
and find their own sentiments and values reinforced. For film programmers antagonistic to feminism but under pressure to screen women's
films, portraits may be less objectionable than films with explicit feminist
themes. The privatization of life in the mid-seventies, whatever its causes
and meanings, creates a hospitable climate for the production and reception of biographical and autobiographical portrait films.

Portrait films encompass a broad range of values and perspectives
toward individualism, reflecting the diversity and ambivalence of the
women's movement. They range from those whose focus is primarily on

the unique and idiosyncratic aspects of a notable woman's life (Gertrude Stein; Louise Nevelson; Alice Neel), to those which emphasize the protagonist's most typical, representative qualities and experiences. The former document the lives of "women worthies," exceptional women whose extraordinary lives are presented as important in and of themselves.[24] The film portraits of Gertrude Stein (*When This You See, Remember Me,* 1969) and Mary Cassatt (*Mary Cassatt,* 1976) exemplify this approach. These films draw on contradictory sentiments and values. They easily mesh with dominant societal values by confining themselves to individual women's extraordinary achievements within spheres traditionally recognized as female. In addition, of course, they appeal to feminist values and sentiments insofar as they dramatize *women's* success.

Most contemporary portraits take a different tack. First, they document the lives of more ordinary, anonymous women who are similar to the filmmaker and to audience members. (In autobiographical films, of course, the filmmakers are the central film subjects.) They depict women whose lives are seen as "representative," not "exemplary" as important to the extent that they reveal and illustrate more universal problems which women face. *Joyce at 34* and *Nana, Mom, and Me,* for example, are both autobiographical portraits of anonymous women which explore conflicts between family and career. In *Home Movie* the young, unknown filmmaker also shows how her life illustrates broader truths, in this case about personal and sexual identity.

The stress on relatively unknown women's lives is partially dictated by necessity. Like all documentarists, feminist filmmakers must rely on people who are willing to donate sizeable amounts of time to the filming process. Subjects are not paid for participation in documentary films. It is far more likely that one can enlist family members or friends in film projects than strangers. In such cases the pre-film "research" is embedded in ongoing interaction between the filmmaker and the potential subject, and the filmmaker does not have to commit material resources to this stage of the project. One well-known portrait filmmaker, two of whose films portray family members (her grandmother and her brother), addressed herself to the financial constraints involved in selecting suitable film subjects:

> We selected them as subjects because I knew them very well. When you have a very limited budget you don't have time to spend months looking for the right subjects. . . . In the case of my grandmother I felt like such a dummy for not recognizing it early. I felt that both of them (here she includes her brother David, the protagonist of her other portrait) had very warm, charismatic personalities that were very *representative.* . . .[25]

There are also important ideological reasons for feminists to portray anonymous women in order to highlight and illustrate typical features of women's experience. The intersection of public and private sides of experience is at the heart of the women's movement. Feminists have been far more interested in untangling the common, quintessential features of women's lives than in celebrating the extraordinary achievements of exceptional women. In highlighting the ways in which individual women reveal significant features of all women's experience, portrait films resolve some tensions between individualism and collectivism, part of the movement's New Left legacy. They transcend "the false dichotomy between the personal and the political, the social and the psychological."[26] They employ what C. Wright Mills called "the sociological imagination," probing the intersection of biography and history.[27]

The following illustrations indicate cinematic strategies for linking the personal and the political.

In *Joyce at 34* several sequences established the filmmakers' views that conflicts between working and mothering typify Everywoman's life. In one scene a number of older women reminisce about the nagging guilt they felt as working mothers with young children. At the end of an animated, almost chaotic conversation, one woman sums up their views by saying, "You aren't really liberated if you walk around with feelings of guilt, and this is I think what many of us [did], right?" Significantly, none of her friends contradict her. The message for the audience is clear. In another sequence the filmmakers suggest, through voice-over narration, that this same conflict existed for an earlier generation of women. Joyce's immigrant grandparents are visualized through old photographs as Joyce says of her grandmother, "She'd been a practicing midwife in Europe but my grandfather wanted her to give it up when they came to this country." The film presents an ambiguous view of the current generation of working mothers. At one point an older woman says, "I think you're truly liberated if you can carry on a career and feel that you're doing the right thing for yourself and for your children." As she says this, the visuals cut to a medium shot of Joyce walking into her film job. The implication of this scene is clear: Joyce (and her generation of working mothers) have succeeded where their mothers failed. The younger women have integrated their familial and occupational roles. Yet other scenes cast doubt on this interpretation. Joyce's conflicts with her husband about the allocation of family responsibilities, like her anxiety when she is away from home on a job, suggest that she, too, like her female forebearers, must continue to struggle with family and career aspirations that are still in conflict.

In the depiction of time in portrait films, one gets a decidedly different view of the meaning of and relationship between past, present, and future than in issue films. Most strikingly, portrait films are not focused on the present. Rather than repudiating the past by ignoring it or depicting it in wholly negative terms, portrait films dwell on the continuities between the past and the present. Frequently they explore a woman's identity through her familial roots.

In two of the best-known portrait films, *Joyce at 34* (1972) and *Nana, Mom, and Me* (1974), it is the filmmakers' anticipation of role changes which triggers the explorations into their pasts.[28] In *Nana,* for example, the filmmaker/protagonist explains that her interest in her familial, especially maternal, past was piqued by her thoughts of having a child. In a self-conscious, didactic scene at the film's opening, Amalie Rothschild looks directly at the audience and says:

> When you start thinking of yourself as a mother, you have to stop thinking of yourself as a child. I see my parents in a new way. I've begun to feel the continuity between generations as well as the change.

Her two earlier films confirm Rothschild's assertion that her views of the past had changed dramatically by the time she made *Nana. It Happens to Us* (1971), her documentary film on the issue of abortion, is structured from a present-minded viewpoint. It depicts women who talk about the horrifying abortion experiences they had gone through. By implication, the film relegates these problems to a barbaric past. By contrast, in *Woo Who May Wilson* (1969), a biographical documentary about an older woman painter, Rothschild dismisses the 62-year-old woman's past in a few sentences. The audience is briefly told of the protagonist's 20-odd-year marriage and life as a housewife and mother in suburban Maryland. The film quickly moves on. Its primary focus is on the new life that May Wilson, newly divorced and on her own for the first time at age 62, is leading as an artist in New York.

In contrast to Rothschild's earlier films, *Nana*'s style reinforces its more positive, even nostalgic, view of the past. Like several other biographical and autobiographical film portraits (e.g. *Libba Cotten, Yudie, Old Fashioned Woman*), *Nana* evokes the past through visual artifacts like old photographs and film footage, and through verbal reminiscences.

Joyce at 34 was the earliest documentary portrait to explore intergenerational relationships. It probed and revealed the roles of, and relationships between, mothers and daughters over several generations. Although made in 1972, when issue films still dominated the film movement, it was tied to newly emerging trends in the women's movement rather than to older themes of generational conflict and a social-problem approach to women's lives.

The first and still one of the best films to explore women's experience and heritage over several generations, *Joyce at 34* opens in Joyce's ninth month of pregnancy as she stares at her swollen reflection in a mirror. Lamenting the endless waiting which her pregnancy forced upon her, Joyce yearns to return to her filmmaking career. The tension between working and mothering is established in the opening sequences and is subsequently documented in Joyce's grandmother's and, especially, her mother's life as the film develops.

After a spectacular birth scene, the film cuts between reminiscences of the past (by Joyce, her mother, and her mother's friends) and sequences of the present. We see Joyce at work, with her family, and in her consciousness-raising group, and we also view several short but effective sequences of Tom Chopra (Joyce's husband) discussing and acting out the working/fathering dilemma in which he has recently been immersed.

The structure as well as themes of the film point to the connections between past and present. *Joyce at 34* was shot over 15 months and uses Joyce's family history to root the protagonist's life and dilemmas in the work and family experiences, traditions, and values of her mother and grandmother. At the same time, Joyce's life was explored and revealed in its contemporary meanings, forms, and possibilities; one was given the hope that Joyce was not just replicating, but was building on, patterns played out in previous generations. Joyce and Tom's relationship, for example, incorporates innovative feminist values and roles. They share responsibilities for child care, and both of them juggle the conflicting pressures from familial and professional obligations; he as a playwright, and she as a filmmaker.

The use of old home movies and family photographs visually reinforce Joyce's interpretations of her family past and female heritage. The audience is introduced to Joyce's mother's mother through her photographs as we are told that she "had been a practicing midwife in Europe but my grandfather wanted her to give it up when they came to this country." Her grandmother quit midwifery, and Joyce's mother also gave up a promising musical career for a more conventional one. She was once a talented musician but decided to become a teacher instead. "Now she only plays once in a while to accompany my brother David who did become a musician."

The film's high point is a luncheon of Joyce's mother's friends. In a very animated, sometimes chaotic discussion, these women vividly recall the guilt which they felt as working mothers. One woman sums up their conflicting, attitudes toward working and mothering in the following way:

> And I always had the feeling if I stayed home, I'm bored and I'm not happy and that's not good for him. If I go to work I come home tired and I don't have any time for him and that's not good for him. Whatever we do is wrong.

As the woman talks, the visuals cut to Joyce, mother of a six-week-old baby, jauntily walking into a filmmaking job. The implication of the editing is clear; it suggests that Joyce (and women of her generation, whose lives she typifies) are resolving feelings of guilt which former generations of working mothers experienced. In many ways, the film sustains the connections between the past and the present; at the same time it hints at new components for the present and future.

Within the feminist film movement, and in the women's movement more generally, there has been a notable shift away from the repudiation of one's early life and maternal past to a search for the complex meanings these have for women's identities. Film portraits enable the filmmakers to search out these meanings in their own or other women's pasts, and enable audiences to witness these explorations.

In autobiographical and biographical film portraits audiences interpret what the film subject's life is like in both rational and emotional terms. Writing about understanding a person's actions in a different context, Max Weber wrote, "Through sympathetic understanding we adequately grasp *the emotional context in which the action took place.*"[29] Weber, of course, stressed the crucial role which empathetic understanding (*verstehen*) plays in allowing us to understand human behavior. He felt that this kind of understanding on the part of the observer differentiated the sociological method from the methods of the hard sciences. Portrait films place heavy stress on empathetic and emotional identifications as well as on rational understanding. By presenting the social context of the protagonist's acts, portrait films elicit explanatory understanding by which "we understand in terms of motive the meaning an actor attaches to [his acts]."[30]

In numbers and emotional impact, portrait films have dominated the feminist film movement since 1974. But the tendency toward portrait filmmaking may already have crested. Several leading autobiographical filmmakers mentioned that they felt this subgenre has been played out and the next step is to make fiction films, or "movies." Scriptwriting appears to many documentary filmmakers as an intermediate step between directing documentaries and directing fiction films, and several filmmakers have written scripts which they hope to sell to producers. The themes, as related to me by the authors, typically concern many of the same issues which autobiographical and biographical documentaries deal with: relationships between the generations, especially women (Miriam Weinstein's script on a Jewish grandmother, mother, and daughter is typical), and relationships between female friends (the theme of Claudia Weill's *Girlfriends,* and of a script written by critic Marjorie Rosen, commissioned by feminist filmmaker Martha Coolidge).

Avant-garde Films

The contextual and collectivized focus of issue and portrait films contrasts sharply with the internal and individualistic criteria normally applied to art objects, including avant-garde films.[31] Avant-garde films are highly individualized artistic expressions which may coincide with feminist themes.

Avant-garde films both depict and "represent" expressive behavior. They emphasize the *emotional context* of action far more than they emphasize the social action itself. Some avant-garde films dwell exclusively on the interior experience, not on social action or interaction. They emphasize the value of expressivity and emotion over cognition. Avant-garde films are primarily valued as personal expressions of their creator's inner emotions and feelings; in this sense, they instantiate expressive behavior and understanding.

Carollee Schneeman's *Plumb Line,* for example, is a film which suggests and represents the filmmaker's search for identity. It features many fragmented, disjunctive images of the filmmaker, in different settings, walking into and seeming to overwhelm the film frame. She moves toward the camera, in an inverse zoom shot, until her face fills the entire frame. The film itself burns and tears apart, echoing the filmmaker's feelings during the end of a love affair. The discordant soundtrack is an aural evocation of the strong sense of pain and disorientation which *Plumb Line* projects. One film catalog describes *Plumb Line* in the following terms:

> *Plumb Line* is a moving and powerful subjective chronicle of the breaking up of a love relationship. . . . The film is a devastating exorcism, as the viewer sees and hears the film approximate the interior memory of the experience.[32]

Another well-known film in this genre is based on the filmmaker's memories and feelings about her own dawning adolescence. *My Name is Oona* is a haunting black and white film composed of fragments which suggest a young girl's emerging consciousness. The girl is the filmmaker's daughter, suggesting autobiographical motifs, as well as motifs concerning female lineage and continuity. The girl is shown riding a horse while she continually, almost compulsively chants "My name is Oona." The repetitive soundtrack becomes, in the words of one reviewer, "a magical incantation of self-realization."[33] Filmmaker Gunvor Nelson discusses *My Name is Oona* in terms that reveal its very private individual meaning for her. When asked about her intentions when she made *Oona,* Nelson replied,

It seems very particular to me, that vision. . . . What I wanted to do was to catch the particular world of my childhood with all the surreal qualities but not in terms of particular subject matter. . . . I wanted the feelings, the atmosphere, the quality of that world I was in and still am in.[34]

The film is difficult to decipher and interpret, and is especially baffling for viewers unfamiliar with avant-garde art. But the soundtrack and the girl's age combine to suggest themes of identity and dawning self-consciousness. Although the film does not provide clear guideposts to its meaning, when shown in feminist contexts it frequently triggers the collective consideration of issues of female identity, and of the difficult passage from girlhood to womanhood. It does not depict the consciousness-raising process, as many feminist documentaries do, but may initiate that process among audience members in the post-film discussion. An individual woman filmmaker's interior experience, reshaped into an avant-garde film, may strike responsive psychological chords among viewers. The women's movement provides a feminist perspective from which films like *My Name is Oona* may be viewed.

But that is not the only possible way in which women's avant-garde films can be approached and interpreted. Many women's avant-garde films are as likely to be shown in theaters which specialize in the avant-garde; in such settings the films are typically approached from a formalist perspective. An emphasis on formal as opposed to thematic elements differentiates avant-garde from documentary films. Rosalind Schneider's triple-screen film, *Parallax* (1973), Carollee Schneeman's self-filmed love-making in *Fuses* (1967), and Gunvor Nelson's eerie soundtrack and haunting use of repetition demarcate these films stylistically. Like the broader modern avant-garde to which they are connected, women's avant-garde films celebrate stylistic innovation. They perpetuate "the tradition of the new."[35] Storm de Hirsch, a leading avant-gardist whose filmmaking career predates the feminist film movement, articulated the importance of personal stylistic innovation.

As an artist I want to make films the way I would like to do them. . . . I am one of those independent filmmakers who is an innovator—I like to explore what can be done. After all, an avant-garde filmmaker likes to improvise, to create his own personal style as an artist. I've developed some of my own techniques, such as etching or scratching on magnetic film. I'm also exploring use of color painted directly onto film.[36]

Avant-garde films by women are more difficult to characterize and summarize than are issue or portrait documentaries. They have different aesthetic assumptions, traditions, and intentions than documentaries and are (at most) tangentially related to feminist ideology.

Women's avant-garde films entail and express the filmmaker's search for meaning. They include those which explore identity, childhood, and sexuality, and others (like those by Storm de Hirsch) which probe more formal problems by experimenting with light, editing techniques, and working directly on the film emulsion. Like related forms of high art, most avant-garde films by women ". . . place high value on the careful communication of mood and feeling, on introspection rather than action, and on subtlety."[37] In structure and feeling they resemble poems. As Maya Deren, one of the founders of the American cinema avant-garde said, an avant-garde film involves the ". . . vertical investigation of a situation, in that it probes the ramifications of the moment, and is concerned with its qualities and its depth . . . not with what is occurring but with what it feels like or what it means. . . ."[38]

Avant-garde films cannot be reduced to consideration of their content. The ways in which their motifs are developed and elaborated are essential to understanding them. In *My Name is Oona,* for example, the modulations in the repetitive soundtrack and the relationship of this seemingly endless verbal and tonal repetition to the dreamlike images of a girl on a horse makes this much more than a film "about childhood and identity," although these are central concerns in the film. *My Name is Oona* is a complex interweaving of sound and image which evokes certain feelings and moods of a particular child and of childhood in general. In contrast to documentaries, avant-garde films do not readily lend themselves to thematic analyses, and hence are tenuously connected to feminism. To many contemporary feminists, avant-garde films, like women's poems and paintings, are considered important as expressions of women's consciousness. Even some of the formalistic avant-garde films which appear to have little to do with feminism have sometimes been claimed by the feminist film movement. It is the fact that these films are made by women, expressing women's "unique sensibility," and not their thematic content *per se,* that explains the incorporation of the films in the women's film movement.

During an extended published discussion of the distinctive qualities of feminist films, one woman filmmaker toys with this idea:

> *Shirley Clarke:*   One of the things . . . about the difference of reading a woman writer and a man writer, if you didn't know, would be in terms of subjectivity.

Though her language is vague, Clarke seems to be saying that women are "more subjective," which she explains by reference to biological underpinnings of sex roles:

Shirley Clarke: . . . the need for men to be transcendental because they do not have within them the reproductive capacity in the same way that women do.
Storm de Hirsch: There's always the biological.
Shirley Clarke: Right, does that not force them in a way to have to think and define things a little bit differently than women?[39]

In many ways the avant-garde filmmaker's prior reputation and connections to women's audiences seem to be instrumental in whether or not her film is defined as "feminist." Those women whose reputations as avant-garde filmmakers were well established before the rise of the feminist film movement were included in the movement from its beginnings. Several leading avant-gardists' films were shown in the First International Festival of Women's Films. (Gunvor Nelson and Storm de Hirsch are the two most prominent examples.) The organizer self-consciously enhanced the Festival's standing in the film world by exhibiting the work of these well-respected filmmakers.

Some other avant-gardists have tried to shape their own reputations by emphasizing the importance of their work to women's audiences. Six New York based avant-garde filmmakers banded together to create a distribution cooperative aimed at tapping the market for women's films as well as avant-garde films. The group, *Women/Artist/Filmmakers*, emphasizes its multiple intentions in each word of its name. Members of *Women/Artist/Filmmakers* all report that they have substantially increased their films' distribution since they formed the group in 1975. They attribute this to the fact that they have legitimized their avant-garde films in feminist terms.

Avant-garde films, lacking distinct, clear-cut themes and narrative structures, do not depict time in comparable ways to issue and portrait films. Avant-garde films involve the vertical penetration of an intense and privileged moment; they revolve around what an experience means or feels like. They exist outside of the dominant Western horizontal conception of time.[40] In presenting an ahistorical, transcendent view of human experience, they implicitly deny the importance of past, present, and future. This further demonstrates their distance from the political world.

In sum, the three major clusters of feminist films express different elements of feminist ideology, and represent different tendencies within the feminist movement. Their changing relationship to the movement suggests some significant shifts in feminist ideology, as well as some unresolved tensions between public and private conceptions of women's lives. Although this discussion has emphasized contrasts rather than continuities among feminist films, the three film types also portray common themes. Pregnancy and childbirth, women's identity, exploitative sexuality, sex-role socialization, and general inequality are central themes in both documentary and avant-garde films. By contrast, sexuality and sensuality are central themes in 13 sample avant-garde films but not in any documentaries (other than those which depict exploitative sexuality). Certain themes are central within the documentaries but absent in the avant-garde films: motherhood/matrilineage, marriage, and work. Table 3 presents a breakdown of major feminist film themes by type of film, e.g. issue, portrait, mixed, or avant-garde.

Table 3.   Sample Films, by Theme and Type[41]

Themes	Issue	Portrait	Mixed	Av. G.	Total
Sensuality/Sexuality	0	0	0	13	13
Identity	2	3	0	6	11
Birth/Pregnancy	2	1	1	4	8
Sex Role Socialization	1	1	4	1	7
Motherhood/Matrilineage	0	5	0	0	5
Exploitative Sexuality	3	0	0	1	4
Marriage	0	3	1	0	4
Inequality	2	0	1	1	4
Work	2	1	0	0	3
Lesbianism	2	0	1	0	3
Abortion	1	0	0	0	1
Discrimination	0	0	1	1	2
Other	4	1	1	4	10
Total	19	15	10	31	75

The following discussion illustrates how these themes are treated within the major genres. The theme of "women's identity" is equally important in documentary and avant-garde films. Some documentaries feature particular women whose lives and identities are emblematic of women in general: *Diane* emphasizes the victimization of women, and *Woo Who May Wilson* emphasizes a woman's ability to transform herself and overcome debilitating elements in her identity, e.g. fear and dependence. Two short films by Liane Brandon, *Sometimes I Wonder Who I Am* and *Anything You Want to Be* focus on general, widely shared problems which women face; the former is a monologue by a woman who feels that her life as a wife and mother is devoid of meaning, and the latter features an adolescent girl who repeatedly lowers her sights and chooses traditional, low-status female roles and occupations—class secretary, not president, and nurse, not doctor. None of the five sample documentaries about identity are autobiographical, while four of the six avant-garde films on this theme are autobiographies. (The other two are films about the filmmakers' young daughters.) The avant-garde films about women's identity are more subjective and intimate and thus are more difficult to summarize. One autobiography, *Plumb Line* (Carollee Schneeman, 1972), suggests the profound impact on the filmmaker's identity caused by the end of her love affair. Another, *Trollstenen* (Gunvor Nelson, 1976) is a very subjective family reminiscence/history, refracted through the memories of the filmmaker.

Themes of birth and pregnancy are also important in both documentary and avant-garde films. Three of the four documentaries on this theme are very matter of fact and didactic; two concern natural childbirth (*Not Me Alone* and *The Birth Film*, which advocates home births) and one is about breastfeeding, *Talking About Breastfeeding*. The fourth film, *The Gibbous Moon*, intimately documents the pregnancy, childbirth, and early mothering experiences of an unmarried woman who chose to have a child by herself. The avant-garde films on this theme are quite different. Three of them are very joyous films which explore the physical/visual dimensions of pregnancy. Gunvor Nelson's *Kirsa Nicholina* focuses on the culmination of a pregnancy; it presents a romanticized view of childbirth in which friends play the guitar and sing during the woman's labor and help with the actual delivery of the baby for whom the film is named. Freude Bartlett's *Women and Children at Large* presents the most joyous and playful view of pregnancy. Two nude pregnant women fill the screen dancing together, as their bellies touch and pull back from one another. Other sequences of the film connect pregnancy to children, thus emphasizing generational continuity. Images of laughing babies precariously sitting up and then falling over reappear throughout the film. One reviewer caught the appeal of this film when she wrote: ". . . the images come fast and surreal, jarring images from a mythic kingdom, where hugely pregnant women rock on and babies fall flat on their face. A really joyous celebration of women, life and film."[42] *Adam's Birth* is the filmed record of the birth of the filmmaker's (Freude Bartlett's) son.

Schmeerguntz is the only avant-garde film on birth and pregnancy which is critical in tone. It contrasts idealized conceptions of pregnancy once paraded by the dominant culture with grotesque views of the bodily changes which actual pregnancy brings. In parts of this film, a woman's nude pregnant body is repeatedly shown in close-up, intercut with images of vomit and swirling feces.

While feminist films, by definition, focus on women, many of them also depict men. Men are a presence in all three types of feminist films. Issue films present men in the most critical light, but even in these there is a considerable range of attitudes. Several issue films carefully distinguish between particular men who have discriminated against or oppressed women and men in general. In *The Woman's Film*, for example, a number of fathers and former husbands of the women in the film come under sharp attack for dominating women, but the film concludes with an appeal for working-class solidarity which clearly includes both men and women. Both *I Am Somebody* (about work and a strike) and *It Happens To Us* (about abortion) feature sympathetic men in important roles. *It Happens To Us* includes more antagonistic than sympathetic men, but by showing a range of male characters this film rejects the inevitability of sex-based conflict. Even *Home Movie,* an autobiographical film about being a lesbian which promotes gay pride, presents the one male in the film, the filmmaker's father, in a favorable (if unimportant) light.

Some issue films do present a negative view of men by consistently criticizing men and praising women. *Woman to Woman* (about general inequality between men and women) is comprised of many different segments, each of which revolves around different kinds of women—industrial workers, housewife/mothers, artists, prisoners, prostitutes, lesbian mothers, and others. In this film there is no attempt to differentiate particular "good men" from men in general. *Three Lives* (about marriage, female identity, and lesbianism) also conveys an anti-male attitude. The two weakest protagonists are heterosexual women who attribute many of their difficulties to men. The third woman is a very lively and appealing lesbian. Implicitly this suggests the vitality of all-female relationships, in contrast to male-female relationships which are shown to be fraught with difficulties.

Many autobiographical and biographical portrait films present men in a sympathetic light. This is not surprising, since these men are intimates (husbands and fathers, usually) of the protagonists. In *Joyce at 34,* the prototypical portrait, Joyce's father is portrayed only briefly in his role as a loving grandparent while her husband Tom is shown struggling with his roles as husband and father. Like Joyce (and many other feminists, including those viewing the film) Tom is trying to combine family and work roles.

Avant-garde films frequently dwell on male as well as female sensuality. Two films depict heterosexual lovemaking (*Fuses, Holding*), and two explore male nudity (*Tulip, Stamen*). Sexuality is a traditional emphasis of avant-garde filmmakers which overlaps with a current interest of feminists.

Conclusion

This chapter has defined and analyzed three major clusters of feminist films—issue documentaries, portrait documentaries, and avant-garde films—and has indicated the relationship of each cluster to the women's movement and to the broader political context. The film clusters express several underlying tensions within the women's movement.

Issue films most clearly reflect the values and orientation of the early New Left faction within the women's movement; they project a social structural, collectivist, future-oriented view of women's lives, focusing on comprehensive considerations of "women's place" and on particular feminist issues. Issue films were commonly made in the early 1970s, when the New Leftists were most numerous and influential in the women's movement as elsewhere in "the movement." Portrait films of particular women surfaced later, around 1974. Film portraits caught the mood of the times; they concentrated more on private, interpersonal experience and less on public issues. They explored the ways that feminist issues were played out in the lives of particular women. For many audiences and filmmakers, these films represented a deeper, more personal exploration of feminist issues. For others they may appeal to narcissistic, escapist urges and impulses. The dualistic, double-edged appeal of portrait films anchors them in different worlds of meaning and sentiment, within and outside of the women's movement. Avant-garde films are more tenuously connected to the feminist film movement. These films may express themes which are consistent with feminist ideology, although none of them were made as "feminist statements" as were most issue films and some portraits. Their acceptance is based on the fact that they were made by women; they are legitimized by vague notions of "female sensibility."

Women's avant-garde films pose the greatest problems for feminist theory. They do not document women's experience, so they can not be enveloped within a mimetic, or realist, theoretical framework. They seem to express women's *unique* "consciousness" or "sensibility," but the cultural determinism central to contemporary feminism cannot (yet) accommodate notions of women's fundamental uniqueness. As long as feminist theory remains tied to cultural determinism, it will be unable to account for, and will in fact obscure, whatever basic differences between women and men may in fact exist.

Three separate feminist film clusters have appeared so far, each with a distinct relationship to feminist values and to tendencies within the women's movement. Since the film movement's beginnings, more varied and personal independent films have been produced by feminists and included in the movement. But the success of the feminist film movement may pave the way for its demise. If most feminist documentarists have their way, they will be integrated into the Hollywood film industry as scriptwriters, cinematographers, and directors. The next expansion of feminist films will go beyond the confines of independent (documentary and avant-garde) filmmaking, into the mainstream. Feminist filmmakers hope to retain their feminist values and insights as they begin making major fiction films which reach out to still larger and broader audiences.

5

Inventing and Routinizing a Market

*The artist thus works in the center of a large
network of cooperating people, all of whose
work is essential to the final outcome.*[1]

Introduction

Contrary to cultural cliches about isolated artists, most art involves a
great deal of cooperation between people performing different, complementary tasks. Film, in particular, involves mundane cooperative activity
in all of its major phases, from production to distribution, exhibition, and
criticism. Differences between these phases in the Hollywood movie industry and the independent film world set the stage for understanding the
institutional support systems of the feminist film movement.

The Hollywood film industry is a profit-making industry which primarily produces narrative, feature movies to be shown in regular movie
theaters. During the heyday of the studio era all phases of the industry
were tightly interwoven: studio producers bought or commissioned scripts,
hired actors and production crews, and arranged distribution and publicity for the completed films, which were then exhibited in theaters which
the studios owned. Although vertical integration of the movie industry
was broken up by law in the 1940s and movie companies were forced to
sell their theaters, in comparison to independent film this is still a relatively integrated industry.[2]

By contrast, the independent film world, in which the feminist film
movement is embedded, is centered in New York and is structurally more
like book publishing than the Hollywood movie industry. Like authors,
independent filmmakers conceive of their films and are the main force
behind the film's production. Most non-theatrical distributors, like publishers, are privately owned, profit-making businesses which typically buy
exclusive rights to already completed films. Distributors occasionally con-

tribute funds to the production costs of a film in process (like an "advance" from a publisher) but, unlike publishing, this is very rare.

Feminist filmmakers created a unique cultural form which, if it was to survive, required unique marketing. Feminist films could not be wholly absorbed into existing marketing patterns; they appealed to distinct audiences which had to be identified and solicited through special means. Confronted with inadequacies in the existing independent film market, several pioneer filmmakers invented distinct ways to market their films, i.e. coops, festivals, and special magazines which focused on "women and film." These innovations were quickly routinized and form the core of the feminist film movement. The invention and routinization of the feminist film market insured the survival of feminist films: it is highly unlikely that feminist filmmakers would continue to produce films if each one had to independently identify an audience and create ways to publicize as well as rent and sell the films.

The two main types of independent films—documentary and avant-garde—have analogies in the publishing worlds: documentary films resemble non-fiction writing and avant-garde films resemble poetry. These basic stylistic differences between film types are reflected in distinctions within each of their major support systems. Documentaries differ from avant-garde films in production, distribution, exhibition, and criticism. Documentaries are clearly the dominant independent form to date. In the documentary mainstream, as in most emergent art movements, the economic structures (especially distribution, but also production and exhibition) developed more quickly and fully than the intellectual, or critical structure.[3]

Avant-garde filmmakers lagged behind documentarists in developing their own economic support systems or using existing ones to help produce, publicize, sell, and screen their films. Accustomed to working alone and faced with fewer opportunities for financial and popular success, they failed to mobilize ways to collectively support their filmmaking efforts. On the other hand, criticism of avant-garde films is more highly developed than criticism of documentaries. Perhaps the avant-garde filmmakers' lack of cohesiveness allowed for the emergence of a more probing, theoretical type of criticism by autonomous (non-filmmaker) critics. The uneven institutionalization of documentary and avant-garde feminist films within the independent film world is a major focus of this chapter.

In the following section the processes of production, distribution, exhibition, and criticism are described within the general context of the independent film world. The discussion then narrows in on the institutionalization of these processes in the past decade of feminist filmmaking. The chapter concludes with an illustrative case history by describing and analyzing the history of one documentary film, *Yudie,* within this institutional framework. In tracing the emergence of the feminist film movement, I hope further to illuminate ways in which a dissident art movement is born and is transformed, or transforms itself, into a new establishment.

Processes

Production

Production/funding, distribution, and exhibition constitute the economic bedrock of the independent film world. Production refers to the material resources (costs and personnel) with which a film is made, as well as defining properties of the film itself, such as its length and whether it is in black and white or color. Documentary and avant-garde films differ substantially in all dimensions of production. In general, documentaries are larger productions than avant-garde films. Independently produced documentaries typically run for about 30 minutes, cost from $3,000 to $10,000 to produce, and involve from 5 to 15 people in various aspects of production (sound, camera, editing), while avant-garde films run from 2 to 10 minutes, cost between $500 and $1,000, and are often created entirely by one person.

Most independent documentarists do not figure labor costs as part of the film, since they often are not able to pay the production crew. Major aspects of costs are film stock, processing, and having prints made. Funding for avant-garde films typically comes out of the filmmaker's pocket or from family or friends. Documentaries, however, increasingly rely on government sources for funding. Public support for film has increased more than sevenfold since 1970. The National Endowment for the Arts (NEA), established in 1965, is the major funding source for independent film in America. The Public Media Program (NEA's film grant-giving agency) grew steadily from 1971 through 1976 from $1.26 million in grants to $7.6 million.

During the sixties, in the first flush of government support for the arts, both avant-gardists and documentarists received considerable support. Eventually the more realistic, didactic, and intellectually accessible documentary films received the lion's share of government funds. Avant-garde films have not received as much government support or public recognition as documentaries have in recent years.[4] (Interviews with filmmakers and film programmers support this conclusion, though I have not been able to find authoritative, published data to document this impression.)

As more money became available to documentary filmmakers, the scale of film projects expanded. Filmmakers who now apply for government support anticipate raising $25,000 or more, for example, and conceive of bigger projects than they did when they had to finance their films themselves by working as teachers, waitresses, or film editors. Larger budgets entail correlative changes in production. More expensive films are typically in color, are produced with larger, more professional crews who are paid for their services, and use more expensive equipment and film processing techniques.

Distribution

Distribution refers to the complex of processes by which a film reaches a market, including publicity, scheduling, shipping, and cleaning and repairing films for sale and rental. It is the only support system in the independent film world dominated by profit-making companies. Private distribution companies like McGraw-Hill dominate the distribution of documentaries, while non-profit associations like the Filmmakers' Coop handle the more specialized, less remunerative distribution of avant-garde films.[5] In addition to private, profit-making companies and distribution coops, there is a good deal of self-distribution: in recent years an increasing number of filmmakers are distributing their own films.

The large profit-making distributors (Films Inc., Time-Life, Macmillan) have annual sales from $500,000 to $10 million and handle from several hundred to 2,000 films at a time, while most small distributors handle fewer than five films and are either self-distributors or are small companies which began as self-distributors.[6] The total market for independent film is estimated at about $25 million annually, divided between colleges, libraries, museums, film societies, government purchases, and other similar users. Probably more than 85 percent of the independent film market involves the rental and sale of documentaries.[7]

Despite the size of the industry on an organizational level, it is unusual for an individual filmmaker to earn a living making independent films. Most independent filmmakers view filmmaking as a part-time vocation with a part-time income; they have other kinds of jobs (often film-related such as editing or cinematography) to earn a living. Distributors normally pay filmmakers either 20 percent of the gross or 50 percent of the net minus expenses which their film generates. Most filmmakers prefer a percent of the gross, because the figures are clearer and the distributor cannot manipulate his costs to cut into the filmmaker's share of the earnings. In this respect, filmmakers distrust distributors in the way authors distrust publishers. It is very difficult to estimate the average earnings of independent filmmakers, but one authoritative source states that most members of New Day Films, a feminist documentary distribution cooperative, earn between $3,000 and $10,000 per year after expenses, while the top earners in New Day make about $40,000 annually.[8]

There is very little commercial distribution of avant-garde films. Instead of commercial distributors like those which handle documentaries, avant-garde films are usually distributed through film cooperatives. The best known of these is the Filmmakers' Coop in New York, which handles nearly 3,000 films made by over 500 filmmakers. Avant-garde coops do not aggressively market the films; they just list the most basic information (title, filmmaker, length, cost, and a one-sentence description) in a regularly updated catalog. As a consequence, only those films which have an independent reputation are likely to be rented through the coops. There is a very wide gap between the most successful and the least successful films handled by these coops. For the number of films which they distribute, the coops do very little business. "In 1976 the Filmmakers' Coop had gross receipts of $88,245 or just under $170 per filmmaker."[9]

Some commercial distributors occasionally handle avant-garde films, particularly those which have topical interest such as films on birth or women's identity. One recently formed feminist self-distribution coop (Women/Artists/Filmmakers) exclusively handles the members' avant-garde films, and another's collection (Iris Films) consists of about one-third avant-garde films and two-thirds documentaries.

Exhibition

Exhibition refers to the conditions and context of the actual screening of a film for an audience. Among independent films, documentaries are much more widely exhibited and reach larger audiences than avant-garde films. Educational institutions and libraries screen documentaries far more often than they screen avant-garde films. This is largely because documentaries are more straightforward, intellectually accessible, and didactic than avant-garde films and thus are more useful as educational resources. Museums and universities (and special regional film showcases) are the primary exhibitors of avant-garde films, but they also screen documentaries regularly.

Nearly all independent film exhibition occurs within institutions which are at least partially funded by the government. Gatekeepers in public institutions are constrained by organized pressure from their constituency, rather than by their own independent reading of the market. Thus non-commercial films by and about feminists are much more likely to be screened in public institutions.

Exhibiting documentaries often means more than just screening a film. Schools and libraries typically provide time and space after a screening for the audience to discuss the film. Current documentaries are open-ended; they are intended to encourage discussions among audience members. The filmmaker, a teacher, or an expert on the topic frequently leads the post-film discussion. Avant-garde films, by contrast, are typically intended and viewed as complete art works in and of themselves. Post-screening discussions, if they occur at all, focus on aesthetic and technical issues rather than on social or political ones.

Criticism

Criticism is the intellectual structure which legitimates an art movement and mediates between the movement and the public. It is somewhat different from the other main components of the independent film world: production, distribution, and exhibition are similar in that concrete processes are involved in the ways in which a film is made, marketed, or shown, while criticism involves an abstract, analytical evaluation of the film product.

Different kinds of critics and criticism are found in narrative, documentary, and avant-garde films. Narrative, feature movies are usually criticized from a "consumer guide" perspective: film reviewers write about movies currently showing in order to help potential audience members select the movies they want to see. Documentary films are typically criticized in a political framework—more for their authenticity and politics than for their entertainment value. Political journals (of social movements and unions, for example) often publish reviews of documentary films which highlight the films' relevance to the politics of their constituency. Thus one finds several left-wing political film journals which regularly publish reviews of documentary films.[10]

Theory has played a more significant role in avant-garde film history than in the history of documentaries. Some of the most important avant-garde filmmakers, beginning with Maya Deren, have written at length on the theoretical underpinnings and implications of avant-garde film. In addition, special avant-garde film critics (e.g. Jonas Mekas and Annette Michelson) have filled the pages of their main journal, *Film Culture,* with their own theoretical musings on the significance of the avant-garde, but little of this reaches beyond the small circle of avant-garde filmmakers and critics. In the brief preface to his authoritative book, *Visionary Film; the American Avant Garde,* P. Adams Sitney alludes to the neglected importance of avant-garde film theory when he writes:

> American avant-garde film theory has received even less critical attention than the films. Therefore I have assumed the task of commenting on the major theoretical

works of the period. . . . The selection of filmmakers to be discussed here has been guided as much by their commitment to the major theoretical concerns as by my original list of films to interpret.[11]

Like the avant-garde films themselves, avant-garde film theory and criticism is esoteric and reaches a small, select audience dominated by filmmakers, intellectuals, artists, and other avant-garde critics.[12]

Institutionalization of the Economics of the Feminist Film Movement: Changes across the Decade

Production of Feminist Films

Feminist documentary films are produced by solo filmmakers, two film-maker partners, or small collectives of feminist filmmakers, while avant-garde films are invariably produced by individual women. Both individualist and collectivist approaches were apparent at the movement's beginnings. A number of feminists individually conceived of their documentary films and were in charge of the various stages of production. A few of the initial documentary films were made by several feminists working together as equals in filmmaking collectives from conception through distribution. Women in San Francisco Newsreel collectively created *The Woman's Film,* while those in New York made *Make Out.* At the same time, a substantial number of women worked with only one partner, which provided them with emotional support as well as economic and other benefits of collaboration on a single project, but did not commit them to working collectively on subsequent film projects.

Films made collectively offered the promise of resolving contradictions between the artistic emphasis on individualism and the feminist emphasis on egalitarian cooperation. Several feminist filmmaking production/distribution collectives were established in the early seventies to provide filmmakers with an opportunity to incorporate feminist values and practices in their art/work. Some of these are Women Make Movies, Tomato Productions, Herstory, and the Women's Film Project.

Feminist documentaries have grown considerably over the last eight years. Documentaries made in 1969 and 1970 were small productions, made on budgets usually well under $5,000 and financed by the filmmaker, her friends, and family. For political as well as economic reasons, the film crews consisted mainly of people who had little or no filmmaking experience. Feminist films created training opportunities for aspiring women filmmakers and politicos who wanted to document feminist struggles.

By 1974 most feminist films were budgeted at well over $10,000 (double the earlier cost) and relied heavily on outside (government) funding. The tremendous growth in federal and some state funding meant that there was considerably more money available for filmmakers, especially women documentary filmmakers, than there had been in 1969. Few women making films in the early period even knew about the existence of film grants, but as feminists redefined themselves as filmmakers they became more aware of expanding film-funding sources and acquired skill in winning grants. Typical budgets for feminist documentary films in 1975 were from $10,000 to $20,000. (By contrast television documentaries typically cost $150,000 per hour to produce.) Films made for $10,000 and more were more professional; they were made by experienced filmmakers who used more expensive equipment, film stock, and processing. Avant-garde films, however, were bypassed by much of the growth in film funding and continue to be funded primarily out of the filmmaker's pocket. Consequently, most avant-gardists continue to make small, inexpensive films with very small crews (often limited to the filmmaker herself). Yet some feminist avant-garde filmmakers, inspired by the documentarists' collectively based success in distribution, joined forces in 1974 to form two distribution groups—Women/Artist/Filmmakers and Iris Films—to collectively promote, distribute, and seek financial support for their films.

Distribution of Feminist Films

Feminists who made films in 1969 and 1970 confronted serious technical and financial difficulties; they rarely thought ahead to how their films would be distributed and where they would be exhibited. If they thought about distribution or exhibition at all, they expected them to follow "naturally" once the film was completed. But in 1970 and 1971 film distributors were blind to the impact on their work of the growing force of the women's movement. Operating outside of the emerging feminist milieu, established distributors were neither personally interested in feminist films nor able to foresee the wide appeal that they were soon to have. Yet women documentarists optimistically approached film distributors with their recently completed films, expecting to be greeted with the same enthusiasm and acceptance which small, sympathetic audiences of women had already expressed.[13] Amalie Rothschild, who soon became a core film movement member, told me she tried unsuccessfully for almost two years to market her first proto-feminist film (*Woo Who May Wilson*, 1969) before she finally joined with several other filmmakers in late 1971 to form a distribution cooperative. When asked what kind of distributors she had approached, she responded with a long list of the standard non-theatrical distribution companies; all of them had rejected her film.

AR: That was in 1969 to 1970. That was before there was a visible women's movement and they had no idea there was any market and they would all say, "Oh, it's a very nice film, dear, but it's not commercial. You understand."

Her experiences typify the situation which most feminist documentary filmmakers faced at that time. Julia Reichert and Jim Klein, co-makers of the now classic *Growing Up Female: As Six Become One* (1971) recounted similar incidents and frustrations. Blocked from existing distribution networks after many months of trying unsuccessfully to market their film, Julia Reichert and Jim Klein reluctantly began distributing it themselves under the name New Day Films. A fourth filmmaker, Liane Brandon, faced parallel problems in marketing her film, *Anything You Want to Be* (1971), which subsequently won top honors at three major American film festivals. Like the other feminist filmmakers, Brandon was patronized and insulted by skeptical distributors. She told how one unsympathetic distributor, having screened her cinematic depiction of the sex-role conflicts and constraints which beset high school girls, advised her to show it at home! When these four filmmakers met, they discovered that they had been working in the same direction and meeting the same resistance.

In the early years filmmakers lacked collective understanding of their situation. Each filmmaker made her film more or less independently, and privately each confronted antagonistic distributors, unaware that others had made similar films and faced similar obstacles in distributing them. Confronting recalcitrant distributors was a radicalizing experience for many feminist filmmakers. As a consequence of frustrated efforts at distribution, opposition to the dominant culture was generalized beyond the ideational level expressed in their films to a broader activist, collective critique. Feminist filmmakers soon realized that they would have to form their own alternative distribution structures if they wanted their films to reach an audience. Some filmmakers joined together in distribution cooperatives while many others individually distributed their own films. Four major feminist film cooperatives were formed by 1975: two were founded in the early seventies (New Day Films and the now defunct Women's Film Coop, both of which primarily distributed documentaries about women's issues and women's lives) and two others were founded after the women's film movement was fairly well established (Iris Films, which distributed both documentaries and avant-garde films, and

Women/Artists/Filmmakers, the only exclusively avant-garde feminist film coop).[14] A number of small local distribution coops also exist.

Feminist film distribution coops play crucial political, education, and pragmatic roles in the film movement. They define the political/ideological significance of feminist films and of the feminist film movement. They also disseminate information about the mechanics of film rentals and sales, and about ancillary activities such as organizing a film festival, applying for film production grants, and organizing other distribution coops. In addition to their political and educational functions, distribution coops do the mundane work of renting and selling feminist films.

Core feminist filmmaker/distributors are spokeswomen for the film movement; they define their distribution activities, like the films themselves, as a form of political opposition to the dominant culture. Their goal is to undermine deeply rooted patterns of sexist thought perpetuated by the mainstream media; this involves an ideational critique of sexist film images and a collectively organized institutional critique of the sexist practices of established film distributors. Core distributors' catalogues serve as manifestoes of the movement. New Day Films, the best-known feminist film distribution coop, states both ideational/intellectual and activist goals in their catalog/manifesto:

> We formed New Day Films in 1972 as a distribution cooperative for films about women. As independent feminist filmmakers, we could see that the women traditionally found on the screen were products of the experiences, imagination, and fantasies of male filmmakers. We were making films based on *women's* needs and experiences. . . .
>
> We formed New Day films because we found traditional distribution channels either inadequate to our needs or inaccessible. Many distribution companies are reluctant to handle controversial films which, while useful, might not turn a high profit. . . .
>
> We found these conditions unacceptable and have set out to create an alternative for ourselves, for other filmmakers, and for audiences. . . .[15]

Iris Films echoes similar views about the oppressive Hollywood images which have confronted women and, by extension, about the necessity to form alternative institutions to produce and distribute feminist culture. One member of Iris summarized their purposes as follows:

> Iris Films is a feminist film distribution and production collective. . . . Iris Films was begun in the spring of 1975 out of the desire to produce and distribute films that spoke to women, in a way that the products of Hollywood do not. We saw ourselves as part of the movement of women to regain, define, and create our own culture.[16]

Members of women's film distribution cooperatives oppose many aspects of the dominant culture. Like other feminists, they are critical of the hierarchical structure of authority which permeates interpersonal relationships among workers in mainstream organizations. They experiment with various alternatives to the hierarchical, instrumental norms which dominate mainstream work groups:

> The three of us had been working together as a collective, and we wanted to continue working that way once we began production of the film. Two of us were experienced filmmakers, and the third, although having no film experience, was very good at interviewing people. We were committed to the idea of sharing skills in our work, and because of this, we decided that each of us would be in charge of an area where she felt the most expertise . . . but that all of us would have an opportunity to work at each of these.[17]

Members of the Women's Film Coop were more polemical in differentiating their work norms from those which characterize the dominant culture. To core members of the Women's Film Coop the interpersonal dynamics of working together, the group process, took precedence over efficiency. Their catalog clearly stated the dominant position on this:

> We want to stress how important meeting outside of your "office" is—we all tend to separate "work" from "enjoying life" but we've found we work a lot more successfully with a minimum of personal formality. The point of which is, if you can't enjoy each other in basic ways, you might as well not try to have collective process.[18]

The history and structure of the feminist film movement are intimately intertwined with New Day Films, the single best-known feminist film group. The history of New Day Films reveals much about the origins of the entire feminist film movement, and about the material and ideological basis of film distribution.

New Day Films

Interaction among filmmakers at the Flaherty Film Seminar in 1971 invigorated New Day Films, a distribution cooperative organized and run by filmmakers who were documenting women's struggles.[19] The founders of New Day had not been able to gain access to existing distribution channels; they were forced to devise an alternative mode of distribution or watch their films die from lack of an audience.

All three early New Day films[20] shared several characteristics which shaped the film movement: they shared a realist orientation and reflected similar political perspectives. All three were issue films which defined women's lives by reference to social structure, not personal qualities inherent in the individual or biological qualities common to women. Thematically, two were about sex-role socialization and women's identity (*Growing Up Female: As Six Become One; Anything You Want to Be;*) and one was a documentary on abortion (*It Happens to Us*). In retrospect it is clear that one of the most important commonalities of New Day's initial collection was that all three films directed their accusations at the structure of sex roles, not at men per se. Parents, teachers, employers, and advertisers, whether female or male, were criticized and ridiculed in the films. Through its collection of films and its widely circulated catalog, New Day helped define the shape of the emerging feminist film movement. Diana Crane, in *Invisible Colleges,* documents the ways that early leaders of scientific movements gain recognition and prominence, in part, by virtue of having their names repeated so often.[21] In a similar vein, the original New Day films and filmmakers were equated with feminist films in general.

During the seventies New Day expanded selectively, incorporating some important new tendencies in the women's movement, especially films about personal, "life style" concerns as depicted in biographical and autobiographical portraits, and films about men's roles. All of the films New Day acquired were documentaries. By the end of 1976 their collection had grown to 13 films including six portraits (*Woo Who May Wilson; Joyce at 34; Nana, Mom, and Me; Chris and Bernie; Yudie;* and *Union Maids,* a political portrait of three union organizers in the thirties) and one film on men's roles, *Men's Lives,* which outrented all the others. *Men's Lives* is the only film on this theme. New Day reflects the increasingly personal and introspective focus of American feminism in the mid-70s. The index in the 1976 New Day catalog lists most films under 6 of the 22 categories. Five of the six most popular categories all emphasize personal dimensions of life: "feelings and attitudes," "growing up in America," "identity," "motherhood and mothers and daughters," "social roles." The sixth is "values in American society."

One very popular new film in their collection is an explicitly political portrait, as closely tied to the standard concerns of the New Left as to the feminist movement: *Union Maids* is a personal/political history of three women union organizers who were active in the labor struggles of the 1930s. *Union Maids* exploits the popularity of the portrait film form yet simultaneously develops political themes which transcend personal issues. One of the filmmakers of *Union Maids,* Julia Reichert, was very active in the New American Movement during the seventies and her films reflect her leftward politics. Reichert has publicly criticized the nostalgic, private view of life projected in most film portraits, and she has successfully attempted to harness this form to her more political interests. *Union Maids* attracted national attention from critics and audiences, but it does not represent a dominant tendency within New Day. Most New Day films reflect the major tendency in the women's movement and in the society—an increasingly personal, not public or political, orientation.

New Day's initial implicit sensitivity to men's roles became an explicit and deliberate focus by 1974. As their initial films show, the founding members of New Day were personally and ideologically receptive to the contributions of men. One of the four earliest members was a man, Jim Klein, a feminist who lived with his filmmaking partner. These filmmaking partners provided money and other kinds of support for *Men's Lives* (1974), a documentary film about men's roles. In 1974 New Day acquired *Men's Lives*, which they publicly justified in political terms:

> Since 1972 many changes have occurred within our cooperative. . . . From lengthy discussions of our concept of what is a "feminist film," we came to feel that feminism is not the domain of women or "women's issues" alone; to us it is much broader. As feminists we are attempting to transform all of society—from daily relationships between people to social, political, and economic institutions. The lives of both women and men need to be explored and changed. So we decided to welcome a film about men and the men who made it into New Day.[22]

New Day does not reflect all changes in the women's movement evenly. It has bypassed certain major feminist tendencies such as lesbianism and contemporary feminist public issues like health care. New Day does not distribute any films which celebrate (or even consider) lesbianism. While some feminist distributors have acquired many films by and about lesbians, New Day has not. Members of New Day were very discreet about their selection policies; they were unwilling to discuss which films they had screened and rejected, or even to discuss the criteria by which such decisions were reached. One filmmaker informant whose film they rejected implied that they were biased against lesbians, a charge which I am not able to substantiate except by circumstantial evidence.

Women's Film Coop

The Women's Film Coop provides an interesting contrast with New Day films. Though it was founded in 1970, before New Day, it never became as successful as its more famous counterpart. This was due, in part, to the time at which it began, its collection of films, and its membership. The Women's Film Coop was founded by three filmmakers in New Haven in 1970, before women's studies courses and programs—the mainstay of the feminist film market—were well established. The Coop had a hodgepodge collection of six films; several of the films were made by men and half of them were avant-garde films only obliquely related to feminist themes and values. It now appears that the more straightforward, explicitly feminist documentary approach embodied in New Day's initial collection of films was more consistent with the aims and orientations of most teachers, librarians, and women's movement groups which rented the films in the early seventies.

The initial members of the Women's Film Coop in New Haven did not even produce a catalog of their films. This is the basic tool of any film distributor, the main mechanism by which distributors communicate with their public. More than anything else, the lack of a catalog indicates the early member's lack of a serious, long-range commitment to film distribution. In 1972 the original Film Coop members dispersed, allegedly to return to making films, not distributing them. A small group of feminists, none of whom were filmmakers, in Northampton, Massachusetts, took over the Women's Film Coop. In contrasting the initial Women's Film Coop members with the women who inherited it, the most obvious and crucial difference is that the New Haven women were filmmakers, while those in Northampton were not. The new members of t ˜ ˜oop were feminist activists who worked without pay, hoping to advance the cause of feminism.

The catalog which they produced provided information about their films, but it also included a declaration of purpose, information about various related aspects of women's films, such as how to organize a film festival, where to rent films about women which the Coop endorsed but did not own, and a bibliography on women's films. All of this was consistent with their self-proclaimed "service orientation." During its middle phase (1972–74) the Women's Film Coop narrowed the meaning of "feminist films" and only acquired documentary films made by women, most of which depicted women's issues from an explicitly political, collectivist perspective. (They continued to distribute their initial acquisitions for pragmatic, economic reasons.) The new catalog and film acquisitions crystallized the political orientation of the Women's Film Coop:

> This catalog is a *critical* selection of films made by women or men, which we feel have a direct bearing on the women's liberation movement, and reflect women's experiences of oppression, struggle, growth, and change.[23]

In its final phase (1975–76) the Women's Film Coop reoriented itself once again; it deliberately stopped distributing all of the films made by men as well as films which celebrated or "endorsed" heterosexuality. The bulk of its final collection were documentary and avant-garde films by and about lesbians. Concern with film style implied in their pro-documentary policy of the middle period was replaced with primary concern for the film and filmmaker's sexual orientation. In a short statement mailed out in 1976, the Women's Film Coop rewrote its history and described itself as "lesbian distributors of lesbian and women's films since 1971. . . ." The Women's Film Coop dissolved in 1976, due as much to the sole remaining member's desire to move on to other projects (especially writing) as to problems rooted in its pro-lesbian orientation.[24]

The two original feminist film coops grew during the seventies. The Women's Film Coop grew from annual sales and rentals of under $100 in 1972 to over $10,000 by mid-1976. New Day grew much more rapidly: in 1972 their combined rentals and sales were around $7,000; by mid-'76 the figure had grown to over $100,000! By 1978 informed sources estimate New Day's annual gross at $300,000. Both groups, of course, acquired new films during the intervening years. The Women's Film Coop collection grew from 6 in 1972 to 16 in 1976; New Day's went from 4 to 13 in the same period. Each coop changed the character of its film collection somewhat, emphasizing specific themes and forms while ignoring others. In general, the distribution structures have become more highly specialized and more clearly defined. These two original coops, New Day and the Women's Film Coop, primarily distributed documentaries. New Day continued to specialize in films about sex roles while emphasizing men's roles more explicitly. The Women's Film Coop moved from a vaguely defined, inclusive "pro-women" position to explicitly political feminist issue films to films by and about lesbians. The two newer feminist distribution cooperatives were formed to handle other kinds of films than those distributed by the two founding groups. As women's avant-garde films were redefined as feminist, two coops were founded to distribute them: Women/Artists/Filmmakers and Iris Films. Iris also distributes documentaries about lesbians.

In addition to the distribution coops, Serious Business, a company owned by a feminist filmmaker, is the major West Coast distributor of women's films. The owner/manager is a woman filmmaker who explained the interconnected changes in her life, career, orientation to film, and the acquisition policies of Serious Business as follows: She began as a "closet filmmaker" in the mid-1960s; her main role was acting as distributor for her husband's avant-garde films. She was very successful in distributing her husband's films, and when they separated she expanded her film distribution efforts. She began by distributing avant-garde films made by a number of her friends who were well-known filmmakers. (Gunvor Nelson was the first filmmaker who Bartlett represented in her fledgling business.) As she became more involved in the women's movement, and more women began making films, her interests unintentionally gravitated toward women's films.

> *JR:*   In terms of your own distribution, do you try especially to distribute women's films? You distribute a lot of women's films now.

> *FB:*   Well, I don't try especially . . . just more and more I like the films by women that I see. . . . Consciously I haven't discriminated that way but I'm more sympathetic to women's films and I make more allowances in a woman's film.[25]

The Serious Business catalog introduces a special section on "films by women" by emphasizing the impact of the women's movement on women's films:

> This special section's emphasis is in recognition of the single most important social change of the last decade: the women's movement and its growth and gains in the search for new perceptions of women's capabilities and value. Film is being used by women as a powerful and artful means of communication: to define, to teach, to entertain, to break down barriers; finally, to move.[26]

In addition to distributing films and defining the movement's ideology, feminist film coops also organize ancillary activities which constitute important parts of the feminist film world. Some coops sponsor major film festivals and "how to do it" meetings on film distribution, and some publish film-related information in their catalogs. The Women's Film Coop held a week-long festival in Northampton, Massachusetts in 1973 which included numerous screenings of feature and short films as well as two full days of panel discussions on the political and artistic significance of feminist films. Iris Films, a combined production/distribution coop, made its debut by sponsoring a major film festival in Washington in 1975. New Day Films and Women Make Movies each sponsored large forums in New York on alternative film distribution. Individual members of feminist distribution coops regularly participate in oral and written public forums on the ideology, politics, and mechanics of feminist film distribution. In addition, all of the women's film cooperatives serve as information centers for women filmmakers, programmers, and others who wish to know more about women's films. Coops distribute information as well as films. They are self-conscious advocates of women's films.

Feminist film distribution coops are flanked by leftist and standard non-theatrical distributors. Many of the standard distribution companies, including those which turned down films by founding feminist filmmakers, now include feminist documentary films in their general collections. These distributors share little of the feminists' sense of mission, but have come to see feminist films as a good investment. As early as 1973 some established distributors recognized the market value of feminist films. Joyce Chopra reported that she and her partner received several offers from established, prestigious non-theatrical distributors who wanted to distribute *Joyce at 34*; the filmmakers decided to join New Day for ideological and financial reasons, but they had distribution choices which earlier feminist filmmakers had not had.

Leftist film distributors accepted feminist documentary films for ideological reasons, when the films coincided with their political orientation. Most left-wing distributors include some feminist films among their more diverse collections. Newsreel, Cambridge Documentary Films, Tricontinental, and Odeon, are all left-wing distributors which distribute feminist films. Newsreel produced and/or distributed some of the first feminist films (*The Women's Film, Janie's Janie,* and *Make Out*) but they subsequently repudiated their early politics and film efforts in favor of a "third world" orientation. Newsreel renamed itself Third World Newsreel and changed from a predominantly white organization to a black and Puerto Rican group, beginning in 1972, and their films reflect this shift. They never actually distributed *Janie's Janie,* and stopped distributing *Make Out,* both of which were quickly acquired by the Women's Film Coop. Occasionally distributors stop distributing films for political or financial reasons; filmmakers then try to secure a new distributor.

Cambridge Documentary Films is another leftist political filmmaking and distribution organization. Its catalog declares that, "It exists as an alternative media resource for libraries, schools, universities, and organizations working for social change," thus linking this small distributor of three films to other general left-wing filmmaking/distribution groups like early Newsreel. Its three films include two feminist documentaries on women's health (*Taking Our Bodies Back: The Women's Health Movement* and *Rape Culture*) which were made by the man and woman cofounders of Cambridge Documentary Films, and a film on health care in China.

In summary, feminist film distribution is a highly developed, diversified support system which includes cooperatives and profit-making companies, and exclusively feminist as well as more general-purpose distributors. In general distributors of documentaries are easily distinguished from avant-garde film distributors. Because feminist film distribution took shape outside of the existing structures, it is the most autonomous of the film support systems.

Feminist film distributors have defined their role in a broad and innovative way. Core distributors do a great deal beyond the nitty-gritty bookkeeping functions normally associated with film distribution. They define the ideology of the feminist film movement; they organize festivals and special showings to publicize the films and promote solidarity among filmmakers and other movement members; and they organize ancillary activities (conferences on alternative distribution and publications on independent film distribution).[27] Feminist filmmaker/distributors established the viability and continuity of the feminist film movement; they made it possible for the films to reach their small intended audiences and for the filmmakers to earn enough money to continue making films which reflect the changing preoccupations of feminist filmmakers and audiences. Finally, their success prompted establishment distributors to include feminist films among their offerings, thus broadening the reach of feminist films.

Exhibition of Feminist Films

Programs at publicly funded institutions, in contrast to privately-owned distribution companies, are vulnerable to pressure from special interest groups. In 1972 and 1973 feminists and women artists in New York demonstrated for equal representation at leading cultural institutions in New York. This led to the inclusion of women's art and films in various exhibits and programs. In the winter of 1973, for example, the Whitney Museum in New York, a gatekeeper and key exhibitor of non-theatrical films, screened over 50 new documentary and avant-garde films by women at a special women's film program. In the same year the New York Cultural Center sponsored a week-long program of women's avant-garde films.[28] Thus, unlike the problems of distribution, feminist filmmakers were not forced to create their own exhibition sites from scratch; they could piggyback on existing non-theatrical exhibitors which served more general purposes. But non-theatrical exhibition presents problems for independent filmmakers, including feminists.

The standard booking and screening arrangements are quite different for independent films than for "the movies." Time and budget constraints typically allow for only one showing.[29] In contrast to continuous, multiple screenings of "the movies," discontinuous, one-shot screenings discourage casual, "drop-in" viewing. This means that non-theatrical films demand more of a commitment in time and planning from audience members than the movies do.

Far more than in commercial movie theaters, there are enormous variations in technical conditions among non-theatrical exhibition sites. The quality of the projector, screen, and even the projectionist, the acoustic and light conditions of the room, and the less obvious but very important "social space" the room creates all vary widely. All of these environmental, "contextual" elements of film exhibition affect the reception that a film generates and receives, but the quality of the "social space" is crucial because feminist films (especially documentaries) ideally generate active audience participation. Most feminist documentaries are intended to raise the audience's consciousness by posing issues and provoking discussions concerning sexism.

Ironically, commercial settings are problematic as well. The physical conditions in the most remunerative and best-attended settings (television and regular movie theaters) are not conducive to the consciousness-raising potential of the films. From an educational or consciousness-raising perspective, the ideal exhibition setting is a comfortable, hospitable space which provides time for post-film discussions. Small rooms with moveable chairs in which non-continuous screenings are scheduled most closely approximate these conditions. Moveable chairs allow an audience to become a discussion group. Even special-interest movie theaters usually have stationary chairs, continuous showings, and closing times which coincide with the end of the last film, all of which preclude opportunities for discussing the films.

Television exhibition, while reaching much larger audiences than would otherwise be possible, all but precludes post-film discussions. Films shown on television reach audiences of individuals or families, and are not usually followed by on-screen discussions of the issues raised in the film. No distributors or filmmakers have rejected theatrical or television distribution because of their less-than-ideal consciousness-raising discussion possibilities, but most feminist filmmakers and distributors are aware of the limitations which various kinds of screening conditions impose.

Despite the limitations of television for such consciousness-raising discussions, feminist filmmakers still see television as very important. Both financially and symbolically, television screenings confer substantial rewards on feminist filmmakers. Typical rental fees vastly exceed those paid for classroom, festival, and similar screenings. Rental fees for classroom use are usually about one dollar per minute while public networks normally pay at least 100 dollars per minute. Commerical networks, which pay 1,000 dollars per minute, never screen feminist or other independent documentaries. In lieu of influential critics devoted to feminist films, television programmers, like some festival and institute programmers, confer prestige and publicity on films and filmmakers. Televised screenings publicly signal one's success within the feminist film world. Films shown on television (like those shown at festivals, museums, and institutes) have greater possibilities of reaching the attention of gatekeepers and of being reviewed in local or national newspapers. In addition, television screenings reach large audiences and publicize a film/filmmaker far beyond the limited, usually word-of-mouth or alternative press publicity which results from school, library, or alternative theater screenings.

An important dimension of television programming for feminist films is the regularity with which the films are shown. Thus far there have been a number of special feminist film events and festivals on television, but almost no regularly scheduled programs. Most of the one-shot programs have been in response to feminist pressures, e.g., direct pressures such as women publicly protesting a station's neglect of their work (Boston demonstration at WGBH, 1973) or the indirect pressure generated by broadly based political actions such as International Women's Year. (The series of women's films shown on WNET seemed designed to defuse women's protests about the station.) As their name suggests, television "specials" are something outside the main program. "Specials" are important in providing visibility for feminist films and the feminist film genre, but critics charge that they are also an effective way of containing the films, of limiting them to occasional and irregular showings.[30]

The major exception to this is "Woman Alive!" a regularly scheduled feminist television series cosponsored by *Ms. Magazine* and a local public television station. From its inception, "Woman Alive!" hired independent filmmakers to produce assigned segments of the shows. The pilot program, for example, included three separately made documentary films on different current topics: a consciousness-raising group, a married couple trying to establish an "innovative" marital relationship, and a segment on the textile workers and a well-known union activist, Crystal Lee Jordan.

Although television and small theatrical screenings are the pinnacle of documentarists' success, to many feminist filmmakers documentaries are still a step below "the movies." Most feminist documentarists expressed a strong interest in making feature fiction films which would be shown in regular movie theaters; consequently while television exhibition is important in its own terms, it may also be a bridge from documentaries to the movies, which remain a primary goal for many filmmakers.

Women's Film Festivals

Established exhibition systems allowed women to screen their films, but did not offer them any control over exhibition. Autonomous feminist film festivals were organized by women as an important adjunct to existing general purpose exhibition. Festivals are extraordinary, irregular showings of a large number of women's films which often feature prominent filmmakers and critics as well as films. In addition to exhibition, festivals serve crucial coordination, publicity, and information functions in the feminist film movement, and impart coherence to otherwise fragmented activities. While other screenings publicize a particular feminist film or a few films, festivals publicize the entire feminist film movement; they inform wider audiences of the existence of a large number of feminist films, introduce them to feminist filmmakers, and disseminate practical information about rental prices and processes. They also promote intramovement solidarity and the collective sense of a movement by introducing filmmakers, critics, and distributors to new works and to each other. (These functions parallel many of those performed by academic meetings.)

The Flaherty Film Seminar in 1971 provided a meeting ground for women who became involved in the First International Festival of Women's Films held in New York in June 1972. In retrospect it is clear that the Festival focused national attention on the burgeoning women's film movement, and provided a model of a type of exhibition which became central to the movement. Kristina Nordstrom, a New York feminist, filmmaker, and film programmer, conceived of the Festival as a way of implementing feminist ideas and energies set in motion during two years of consciousness raising. Nordstrom had conceived the idea for a women's film festival after hearing about a Mae West film showing organized by New York Radical Feminists. Frustrated by the quietistic, introspective politics of consciousness raising, she began thinking about ways to organize a showcase of women's films. In her words:

> We had been in a consciousness-raising group and I was tired of just talking. I wanted to do some kind of action. . . . I had worked for the New York Film Festival . . . and I knew the steps of organizing a film festival. . . . I knew there had been some films made by women but I didn't know how many. And I thought a festival of women's films would really spotlight that for women and be something positive that they could identify with and encourage more women to do it and convince the world at large that women have those kind of capabilities so that they could get more work. . . . I drew up a proposal, I started calling up people to ask them to be sponsors, and then I went to Flaherty.[31]

The group of women who met with each other at the Flaherty on International Women's Day, 1971, responded to Nordstrom's suggestion that they help plan a women's film festival; the Flaherty "women's group" became the core of the screening committee for the proposed festival. In addition, women from Nordstrom's consciousness-raising group were very actively involved in many aspects of organizing the Festival. They raised money, handled correspondence, wrote program notes, arranged publicity and "hospitality," as well as helped screen and program films. The Flaherty women, on the other hand, were solely involved in screening and evaluating the films.

This division of labor finally proved to be unsatisfactory to the majority of women on the screening committee. In particular, they were dissatisfied with having such a circumscribed, fragmented, advisory role in which they were powerless to make decisions about the entire Festival. Like many feminists at the time, many of those working on the First International Festival of Women's Films fought against the centralization of authority. They argued for an organizational form more in keeping with feminist principles of "decentralization" and "participatory democracy," and resigned en masse when they realized they were losing the battle with the Festival director.

The screening members published their letter of resignation shortly before the Festival opened; in short, they accused the director of hoarding power:

> In order to perform this task (selecting films) well, it was necessary to have a clear concept of the motivations, goals, and related managerial policy of the Festival. Although the screening committee sought repeatedly to have these areas defined and to translate them into a working structure, we continually encountered on the part of the Director an attitude that these issues should not concern us. Realizing the Festival's cultural importance to women, we felt we could not simply continue looking at films while these matters were left undetermined.[32]

Nordstrom saw the situation quite differently, as she revealed several years later in an interview. She did not publish a response at the time, feeling that such public disputes would adversely affect the Festival. According to Nordstrom, the dissident members had been unwilling to do much of the humdrum routine work connected with organizing the Festival but they were equally unwilling to accept the restrictions which this imposed on their authority. Interestingly, none of the nearly 20 women on the screening committees for the Second International Festival of Women's Films, held four years later in 1976, objected to a similar organizational structure. In part it was because the screening committee was itself selected with past conflicts in mind. But another explanation is at least as plausible: the fervor which once surrounded issues of decentralization had dissipated considerably by 1976.

The two international festivals held in New York in 1972 and 1976 tower above the many women's film festivals organized to date. Each of these festivals included more than 100 films mainly from the United States, Canada, and Europe—far more than are typically included in women's film festivals. In addition to screening the films, the festivals held daily press screenings, presented extensive panel discussions, published program notes, and, in the case of the Second Festival, organized related conferences on "Making It" in the film world and on feminist film scholarship. These festivals succeeded in focusing national attention on women's films.

The First International Festival of Women's Films presented an enormous number and range of films directed by women: 83 programs consisting of 125 films (feature films, animation and industrial films, documentaries, avant-garde) were screened and panel discussions on related topics were held (e.g., the image of women in film, female scriptwriters, etc.).[33] In the words of one contemporary reviewer, "Even film scholars were amazed to discover that there were three weeks worth of films directed by women in existence."[34]

Significantly, a wide range of films was selected for screening at the First Festival. All of the Festival organizers agreed from the outset that none of the then prominent ideological tendencies within feminism would dominate the Festival. All films directed by women were eligible. Films of all styles, featuring all kinds of subject matter, were seriously considered for inclusion in the Festival. This proved important because the Festival was the "debut" of the feminist film movement, and was therefore important as a pacesetter in defining what followed in its wake. For quite some time, the program notes from the Festival (widely circulated during the Festival, and mailed to hundreds more who requested them after the Festival was over) were the only published information on feminist films.[35] They were the first comprehensive definition of and guide to this emerging movement; they allowed people who had missed the Festival (teachers, film programmers, filmmakers, critics, etc.) to learn about the films and the film movement. Films shown in the Festival were publicized, and those which were not shown were (at least temporarily) written out of this new film world. In spite of their catholic intentions, however, the Festival programmers were more receptive to documentary films which explicitly concerned women and women's issues than they were to avant-garde films. Two well-respected avant-garde filmmakers (Carolee Schneeman and Milena Jelinek) were excluded from the First Festival, although no major documentarists were excluded.

Many women's film festivals around the country followed the First International Festival of Women's Films. Festivals became the major forum for exhibiting/introducing a great number of women's films to an audience in a relatively short time. Typically held at colleges, museums, and alternative theaters, women's film festivals usually last from one day to one week; programs are screened only once and interested people can view a good deal of work (new to them, if not recently completed) in a compressed period.

It is impossible to determine exactly how many women's film festivals have taken place because many, especially those held in university towns, were only publicized locally. Kristina Nordstrom, director of the two largest festivals, estimated that at least 40 to 50 festivals occurred between mid-1972 (after the First International Festival of Women's Films) and late 1976. During those years major festivals were held in Boston, Philadelphia, Washington D.C., Chicago, San Francisco, Los Angeles, Jacksonville, Florida, and Northampton, Massachusetts.

The Second International Festival of Women's Films was held four years after the first in New York. In spite of the popular success of the First Festival, demonstrated by the audiences' enthusiasm and by the many other festivals which it inspired, Kristina Nordstrom had a difficult time raising money for a Second International Festival. Funds totalling $62,840 were eventually raised from government agencies, box office, and individual donors. This sum fell far short of the budget, which had been projected at $95,000, though Kristina Nordstrom and her coorganizer, Leah Laiman, spent considerable effort during the year before Festival II trying to raise money from various state, federal, and foundation sources, as well as from private businesses and individuals. Many people, however, seemed to share the views of a leading feminist film critic, Molly Haskell, who had strongly supported the First International Festival but questioned the need for a second one.

> The subject of women in the cinema . . . has become a staple of college syllabuses and cocktail party conversation and mass media featurettes. Even Hollywood seems to have gotten the message, which means that it's certainly too late for us to be talking about it here in New York. By the same token, the Festival of Women's Films may be an idea whose time has come . . . and gone.[36]

The Second Festival was a major cultural spectacle in New York, less an alternative event than the first. It was well attended by critics and the larger film-going public. A party at the French Embassy trumpeted the opening of the Festival; Jeanne Moreau's directorial debut, *Lumière*, lent it additional glamor and publicity.

The Festival sponsored two important new ancillary activities, a three-day conference on producing documentary and feature films and a one-day conference on feminist film scholarship. The career-oriented conference was heavily subscribed in advance of its opening. Many of the women who attended had been active participants in the women's film movement for several years, but wished to "make it" in the mainstream, while others were aspiring filmmakers seeking to learn some practical information about producing documentaries or entering the mainstream film industry.

Like the conference on production and distribution, the scholarly conference was the first of its kind. The papers and panels included such topics as popular feminist film criticism, women's roles in the mainstream movies, the relationship of the cinéma vérité aesthetic to women's issues and feminist values, Maya Deren's aesthetic vision, ethnic dimensions in women's films, and pedagogic approaches to teaching women and film. Nearly all of the papers which were submitted dealt with either fiction films ("the movies") or documentaries, not the avant-garde. At this conference, as in feminist film criticism in general, there was a decided lack of theoretical underpinnings for women's filmmaking efforts.

Film festivals are one well-developed component of the feminist film world. They are very useful in terms of the publicity and visibility which they provide, but they are problematic as a major exhibition/publicity network. Films must be solicited, screened, evaluated, and programmed. Funds must be raised for a variety of expenses. Bookings, publicity, live presentations by filmmakers, and "hospitality" must be carefully coordinated. All of this "start up" effort is expended in a short time, usually two days to one or two weeks. The energy and knowledge which go into, and grow out of, any particular film festival are then scattered to the winds. Most feminist film festivals are organized by women with little or no experience; they are one-shot events for the organizers.

Although many feminist film festivals and special showcases have been quite successful, their organizers soon became aware of the limitations of one-shot screenings. Popular support for a film did not have a chance to build up if the film was only shown once or twice. The full acceptance of feminist films required that their distribution and exhibition be more routinized. While occasional festival and museum screenings may introduce some interested people to the films, they are not enough to generate an audience/market which is steady enough to keep the film movement afloat. The women's movement, institutionalized in the college classroom market, especially in psychology, sociology, and women's studies courses, provides the steady support which the film movement needs to sustain itself.

Audiences

Who are the audiences for feminist films and how do they respond to the films? By all accounts college students constitute the great majority of the feminist film audience. All distributors questioned reported that student groups comprise at least 75 percent of their market.[37] I spoke to the following filmmaker/distributors about this: Freude Bartlett of Serious Business Company, Joyce Chopra and Mirra Bank from New Day, Eric Breitbart from Odeon, and Rosalind Schneider from

Women/Artist/Filmmakers. More than anything else, the institutionalization of the feminist movement within colleges and universities has created a new market for feminist resources.

In order to gather additional information about audiences, in 1975 and 1976 I asked six audience groups at a range of exhibition centers (museum, "art" theater, film festival, college classroom, and specialized repertory movie theater) to fill out questionnaires about their relationship to feminism and to film, and about their reactions to the films they had just seen. (See Appendix B for questionnaire.) The total number of audience members is not known, but I would estimate that the response rate was between 75 and 80 percent.

The respondents were distributed as follows: non-classroom audiences (festivals, special theaters, and museums) consist primarily of non-art professionals (35.7 percent), most of whom were teachers and social workers, students (26.1 percent), followed by filmmakers (10.9 percent) and other artists (5.2 percent). (Only two small college classrooms were included, and consequently students were underrepresented among the sample respondents.) These three audience groups (professionals, students, and filmmaker/artists) do not differ significantly in their response to feminist films or in their rate of feminist organizational membership.

Ages of feminist film audiences in this study are typical of film viewers in general, i.e. people in their twenties and thirties. Eighty-three percent of the audience members were under forty. As one would expect, women far outnumber men at feminist film showings. Of the 230 respondents, 186 (81 percent) were women. The questionnaire did not reveal any distinguishing characteristics about the male audience members. Perhaps many of them had accompanied women friends, but unfortunately the questionnaire did not elicit this information.

Of the "voluntary" audience members who attend open screenings, how many closely identify with feminism, and how many identify with the independent film world? To what extent do these identities overlap? Is there a substantial part of the audience for whom both feminism and independent film are important, or is the voluntary audience divided among two distinct types, feminists and "film people"? In order to investigate this issue, respondents' feminist organizational involvement and attitudes were analyzed in relation to their involvement with movies. (Those who designated themselves "fan," "critic," and/or "(aspiring) filmmaker" were labelled "film people.")

Those who belonged to feminist organizations were much more likely to have seen such films before.[38] Here again, feminist participation seems to overlap with film participation; these do not constitute two distinct kinds of interests. Rather, film has become a major medium of the new feminist consciousness, and, more recently, feminism has become a legitimate theme for independent film. Similarly, organizational affiliation is also correlated with respondents' evaluations of the movies. Respondents were asked what they "liked" and what they "disliked" about the films. In answering the former, "What do you like most about these films?" the viewers who belonged to feminist organizations were much more likely to express feminist values and attitudes, which clustered around four major subthemes: "honesty/realism," "strengthening," "focus on women," and/or "politics."

In light of the high overall response rate to the questionnaire, it is surprising that so many people completely bypassed this pair of questions, failing to indicate what they liked, and, especially, what they disliked about the films. Forty-one people (17.8 percent) did not respond to what they liked, while 120 (52 percent) failed to indicate what they disliked about the films. While this may reflect the difference between these more "demanding," open-ended questions, in contrast with the other forced-choice questions, it may also be part and parcel of the pervasive anti-critical bias of feminism and the feminist film movement.

"Feminist attitudes" correlated with the likelihood that viewers had seen similar films before. As one would expect, those with the most pro-feminist attitudes were much more likely to have seen several feminist films than those who did not share these attitudes. This is consistent with the finding about feminist organizational behavior, another indicator of feminist posture. By 1975 and 1976 when I surveyed these audiences, feminist film viewers, like filmmakers, did not relate to the films as *either* feminist *or* filmmakers. Audience members had become enmeshed in the evolving feminist film world, a world in which feminism and film overlapped, as had feminist filmmakers. It is likely that earlier, in 1972–73, most documentaries by and about women were viewed primarily by feminists who had little or no other connection to independent film. Women's avant-garde films in those years were primarily screened at avant-garde showcases and viewed by other filmmakers and artists, not feminists. The emergence of audiences of women (and some men) interested in both feminism and women's independent films, an outcome of the festivals, conferences, and related publicity/outreach efforts, helped ground the feminist film movement more firmly in the world of independent film.

Criticism

Criticism legitimates an art movement and mediates between the art movement and the public. In most older arts the support structures are well differentiated and evenly developed; artistic, economic, and critical roles are performed by different people with different kinds of training and different interests. In new arts, however, artistic, critical, and economic functions are typically fused and intertwined. Ironically, it is emergent fields of artistic activity which exhibit the greatest status problems and hence the greatest need for abstract, verbal constructions which explain and legitimate the new activity to the outside world.[39]

Feminist film critics can be divided between those primarily oriented toward Establishment movies (Hollywood and European features) and those oriented more toward feminist documentary and avant-garde films. (Non-feminist critics also review feminist films.) Establishment critics write for general circulation establishment journals and focus on women's roles in mainstream movies. There are two core critics, Marjorie Rosen and Molly Haskell, and about two or three others. Most establishment feminist film critics began their careers in the late sixties as general film critics began their careers in the late sixties as general film critics. With the rise of the women's movement they became interested in feminist issues, an interest which they incorporated in their film criticism. Both core critics, for example, had worked as film critics for several years before they published well-known books on women and the movies, books which established their reputations as preeminent feminist film critics.

Establishment-oriented feminist critics have not become major spokeswomen/apologists for feminist films. They continue to define themselves primarily as film critics, "not just feminist film critics," in one woman's words. They resent being "ghettoized," and want to review the entire range of films which their male counterparts review. Unlike feminist filmmakers who began making films as a way of expressing their political values, critics subsumed their interests in feminism under their stronger, more general interests in film criticism. The critics' ambivalence distances them from the ideological core of the feminist film movement. As a result, they do not consistently apply feminist perspectives to their film criticism.

Establishment critics, in emphasizing Hollywood and European movies, have neglected feminist films. Institutional constraints are at least as important as professional ambitions in explaining the critics' interests and their relative neglect of feminist films. Essentially, one cannot make a living by only reviewing feminist films. The most remunerative feminist film criticism is sporadically published in establishment journals, and the criticism must conform to the journals' overall orientation to the dominant culture. The most important type of film criticism in this country is the "consumer guide" variety. Film reviewers are expected to help potential audience members select the movies they want to see. Critics thus write about movies that are currently playing so their readers can make more highly informed choices. Feminist films appear infrequently, are shown irregularly, and cannot be easily incorporated in the consumerist approach. Though establishment journals have not been the consistent locus of innovative feminist film scholarship or criticism, they have to some extent popularized feminist views of the dominant culture. In doing so, they mediate between the views of the women's movement and those of the wider society.

Non-establishment criticism is oriented either toward documentary or avant-garde films. Like the films themselves, these two strains of criticism are quite distinct. Documentary criticism tends to be descriptive, concrete, and personal, while avant-garde criticism is more analytical and theoretical. For feminist documentary films, like photography, the roles of practitioner and of theorist have not yet been differentiated. Women documentary filmmakers, especially those centrally involved in distribution, have usurped the roles which critics play in more established arts. They define the ideological meaning of the feminist film movement as a whole, and interpret the aesthetic and political meaning of individual films (especially their own) to audiences. It is far more common for a filmmaker or filmmaker/distributor to lead a post-film discussion, for example, than it is for a critic to do so. Feminist filmmaker/distributors set the tone for documentary film criticism, which is generally concrete, descriptive, and personal, not analytic. Documentarists typically focus on their autobiographical connections to a film's themes, their careers as women filmmakers, and (with filmmaker audiences) technical issues about the production process. What's lacking here is a probing and analytical approach which looks critically at the assumptions and implications of the films as women's films.

Most feminist film critics manifest these anti-theoretical assumptions. There are three major guidebooks to the feminist film movement, all of which provide straightforward programming information about both documentary and avant-garde films (running times, summaries of major themes, rental sources and costs) without including theoretical or political analyses of the films.[40] These books were published in 1973–74 and reinforce the concrete and descriptive approach to the films noted earlier. They function as consumer guides for film programmers just as regular movie reviews function for potential audience members. In *Women in Focus,* the one guide book which includes critical comments, Jeanne Betancourt, the author, lodges her criticism between a summary of the "story" and personal comments by the filmmaker. The "critical" comments are explicitly aimed at the information needs of librarians, and teachers, as Betancourt states in her introduction:

Librarians have here a guide for new purchases—where and how to use them. College and high school personnel have a manual that helps them determine how to use their audiovisual funds without spending the hours to search out films as I have.[41]

Women in Focus also indicates each film's connections to feminism by concluding the discussion of most films with a bibliography of "Suggested Feminist Readings." The text on *Joyce at 34,* a film on women's conflicts in combining work and family roles, for example, is followed by a list of 10 readings which includes analytical works such as Jesse Bernard, *The Future of Marriage,* Cynthia Fuchs Epstein, *Woman's Place,* and Ann Oakley, *Sex, Gender, and Society.* Instead of developing a theory of feminist film, this critic implicitly views feminist films as illustrations of existing feminist theory and thus refers her readers to relevant theoretical works.

This illustrates the general connections between feminist documentary film and feminist theory: documentaries are intended to reflect elements of feminist theory, not to explore or generate new, innovative feminist theories. Historically, this has been the typical relationship between documentary film and political movements. William Nichols's comments on the relationship between Newsreel and the New Left are equally applicable to the feminist film movement in relation to feminism: "Newsreel acts as a barometer, not a vanguard, of the New Left."[42]

There are several reasons why no adequate theories of feminist documentary film have yet emerged. Theory and criticism fundamentally contradict major premises of feminist ideology. Many feminists have implied or argued that women's creative efforts should be encouraged and supported by praise. In rejecting the highly competitive and critical aspects of typical male behavior, some feminists have totally rejected the possibility of criticism.

Documentary films present critics with additional problems. For most critics it is very difficult to separate a documentary film as a political/aesthetic creation from its subject. This is especially problematic with portrait films, where criticism of the film as a cultural creation is taken (or meant) as criticism of the protagonist's character. There is a fine line between criticizing a film about a woman's life and criticizing the woman herself. One prominent critic, tired of struggling with this dilemma, pleaded for fictional films based on ". . . revelations for which the filmmaker rather than the interviewee is responsible."[43]

One critical camp veers sharply from this anti-theoretical tendency. There is a small but increasingly important group of feminist academics and intellectuals grounded in feminist theory as well as in film who are struggling to explore the distinctive, unique parameters of women's culture. These women, whose work is highly theoretical and appears in occasional feminist or film journals and is at the heart of the new feminist film journal, *Camera Obscura,* have focused more on women's avant-garde films than on documentaries. Indeed, some of them argue the heretical view that only avant-garde cinema has any possibility of being feminist.[44] Mimetic, realistic cinema, whether fiction or documentary, uses available, hence necessarily patriarchal, cinematic structures, and therefore perpetuates sexist ways of seeing and conceptualizing the world.[45] Avant-gardists, according to some of these critics, can operate in a genre freer of convention and thus closer to the bone of female experience.

The implicit underpinnings of a theory of distinct, sex-linked linguistic and conceptual structures derive either from biological explanations or from explanations rooted in millennia of cultural traditions. Feminist film critics have not yet begun to *explore* the sources of the differences which they are trying to identify, but it is likely that their criticism will move in this direction. Questions concerning the ultimate sources of sex-role differences are currently at the forefront of feminist scholarship.[46] These questions concerning distinctive female cultural forms have been central to feminist art critics for several years. Questions about female sensibility and female imagery dominate the most important and popular feminist art criticism.[47] Perhaps the dominance of the documentary aesthetic and the correlative rise of documentary filmmakers as critics impeded the development of a serious, theoretical feminist film criticism. As a number of documentary filmmakers move into fiction filmmaking, the dominance of the documentary aesthetic may wane, allowing room for more analytical criticism to emerge.

Conclusion by Way of an Example: The History of a Feminist Film

The life history of one feminist documentary, *Yudie,* will illustrate the workings of the support systems at the core of the feminist film movement. *Yudie's* long journey from conception through production, distribution, and exhibition, and the critical responses which it called forth, are explored in order to delineate the complex interconnections between the different support systems and a specific film.

The way in which *Yudie* was financed and produced had important implications for the final film. The filmmaker, Mirra Bank, initially intended the film to illustrate the strength and determination of her aunt Yudie, an older Jewish woman who transcended conventional sex-role expectations by remaining single and living alone. As Bank shot and edited the film over a period of two and a half years, however, it became less polemical and evolved into a much more delicate, poetic film about its central character. These changes from original conception through completion reflected the political and personal changes which the filmmaker went through during the same period. *Yudie* was made so slowly because the filmmaker financed the film herself and repeatedly ran out of money. She continued working as a film editor and waited until she had saved enough money to buy more film and/or have it processed.

Although Mirra Bank had been working as a film editor for several years before she began making *Yudie,* she had not made any independent projects and she did not then think of herself as a filmmaker. In her words, "I never even began to think of myself as a filmmaker until someone else called me that."[48] This meant, among other things, that she was not aware of various government and foundation grants with which she might have financed her film. Being unaware of funding sources was not unusual for women making their first independent films in the early seventies; most of the early feminist films were paid for by the filmmakers themselves, often with money borrowed from friends or family. As Bank points out, "When I first started working on this film, I really didn't even know about grants. Not only that, but there weren't that many grants available."

The production crew for *Yudie* was very small and relatively inexperienced. Bank did much of the work herself; she directed and edited the film, and she also photographed the stills of New York which punctuate it. The remainder of the production crew included two men just out of film school (one on camera, one on sound) and a woman who worked as assistant camera person. Economic constraints further meant that *Yudie* was shot in black and white which, at that time, was substantially less expensive than color film to buy and process. The fact that this was a documentary film about a single subject also made it simpler and cheaper to produce. Bank used editing facilities at her various jobs to cut the film on week nights and weekends. During this protracted process, she learned a great deal about documentary filmmaking and about this particular film:

> I would carry the film around as it grew from job to job and cutting room to cutting room . . . and really what happened was a kind of forced education about that kind of filmmaking which I wouldn't have had had I been wealthy enough to just go out and shoot it.

As the film project was drawing to a close Bank applied for a grant from a state arts council, but she was not awarded the money and finished the film while she was on unemployment compensation. (This is occasionally used by filmmakers and other artists as though it were a government grant for art projects.)

Exhibition, Criticism, and Distribution

Yudie was finally completed in the summer 1974, just in time to enter the prestigious New York Film Festival. Although the Festival rarely shows small documentaries, the judges responded enthusiastically to *Yudie* and incorporated it in a documentary program on ethnicity which was being assembled. Exhibition at the Festival definitely launched *Yudie* as a successful feminist film. It was reviewed in major gatekeeping publications (e.g. the *New York Times*) and also directly reached influential audience members. Just after the New York Film Festival, Bank reports:

> I was contacted by Channel 13. I had just finished working at "13" (as an editor on the series, "The Men Who Made the Movies"). Bob Kotlewitz . . . contacted me about wanting to show the film on "13." I said great *but I want to be hired to make some films as well*.

Directly and indirectly, then, the Festival screening opened other opportunities. Channel Thirteen acquired *Yudie* and hired Bank to make two more films. Subsequently, the film was acquired by other local public stations and by PBS (the national Public Broadcasting System). Sales totalled about $6,000 or $7,000 the first year, even before it was officially in distribution. As Bank herself noted, *Yudie* turned out to be ideal for television; it directly treats themes with wide audience appeal: aging, women, ethnicity, and city life.

At the public television seminar in 1975 (a yearly national meeting for television workers to learn about new "products") *Yudie* was screened and won a good deal of attention. This too, like the Festival described earlier, was important in terms of rentals and sales. Other key screenings, like one at the Educational Film Library Association's annual American Film Festival and another at the Chicago Film Festival, helped further *Yudie's* reputation during its first year.

Although all of these festivals and screenings created clear opportunities for favorable publicity and successful marketing, Bank did not persistently follow up on the opportunities. Like many feminist filmmakers, she was more interested in making new films than she was in distributing one she had completed. She was not willing to devote to distribution the full year which it usually takes to successfully launch a film in the independent film world and the feminist film movement. She did not take the lead in defining the film's meaning, either by giving frequent interviews or by supplying critics with quotable promotional materials which could fill out their reviews. Mirra Bank's minimal publicity efforts on behalf of *Yudie* explain in part why reviews were often shorter and less developed than reviews of other feminist films on "women's heritage" which appeared at the same time. She did not, in fact, even decide on how to distribute the film for over a year after it was completed, although she had been approached by New Day Films and by commercial distributors as soon as *Yudie* premiered. She was not ready to take on all of the work which self-distribution within New Day entailed, but had serious reservations about handing it over to a commercial distributor and "alienating myself from such a personal film which I had worked on for so long." Mirra Bank's ambivalence about accepting the responsibilities which New Day entailed, and, on the other hand, about "abandoning" her film to a commercial distributor, kept *Yudie* out of formal distribution for a year. She finally joined New Day because she felt it was the "morally correct thing to do." Once in distribution, *Yudie* reached the normal, standard New Day market—mostly university classes and film programs and some community groups. Bank never cultivated any of the obvious special markets which the film clearly appeals to—Jewish groups, and groups concerned with aging.[49]

Yudie does not spell out preexisting tenets of feminist ideology, and thus poses special problems for film reviewers. Intrinsic qualities of the film itself make it more difficult to review. Unlike many feminist documentaries, *Yudie* is suggestive, delicate, and poetic, not didactic. Mirra Bank put it very well when she said, "It gets in and out of its statements in an unobvious way which means there's less to hook into." Like the feminist film movement, the analysis of *Yudie* awaits the development of a theoretical feminist film criticism.

6

Conclusion

Feminism into Film has delineated the emergence and development of the feminist film movement which includes feminist films and filmmakers and the special feminist film market. Independent film in America and the contemporary feminist movement provide the broader historical and political contexts in which the feminist film movement developed. This chapter begins by briefly summarizing and highlighting the significance of the ground which has already been covered, focusing heavily both on the tensions between personal and political life which underlie and animate feminism and independent film and on the implications of the autonomy of the feminist film movement. The chapter concludes by anticipating the future course of the historical development of the feminist film movement.

In looking back over the ground covered in this study, I find one of the most striking features to be the extent to which feminism and independent film pulsate with the same tensions.

The feminist film movement reverberates with and expresses the fundamental tensions within contemporary feminism between public, political behavior, on the one hand, and private experience on the other. Similar tensions pervade and inform the independent film world: documentary and avant-garde films embody public and private emphases respectively. In addition to the thematic and stylistic differences which distinguish them, the two film forms are created by distinct groups of filmmakers for different, though overlapping, markets. The particular resonance of feminist films is a consequence of these parallel tensions.

Contemporary feminists, in contrast to earlier ones, attribute as much significance to personal life and interpersonal relationships, such as marriage, women's consciousness, sexuality, and motherhood, as to traditional political concerns with legal equality.[1] In its current phase feminism is a multi-issue movement, seeking major reforms in political, economic, legal, familial, and sexual spheres. In addition to challenging sexism within each distinct institutional arena, feminists have recognized the interpenetration of these spheres. The slogan "the personal is political" conveys contemporary feminists' preoccupation with personal life and their at-tempt to redefine and legitimize personal issues as properly public concerns.[2]

Initially, public and private tendencies were isolated within distinct branches of feminism; the older branch tended to emphasize traditional public, political behavior and issues, while the younger branch, especially the "radical feminists," emphasized personal identity and interpersonal relationships. Unification of the older and younger branches of feminism meant that tensions between private and public orientations are no longer isolated or so sharply posed in distinct wings of the feminist movement, though they do continue to exist.

Basic thematic shifts in feminist documentary films illuminate parallel shifts in the public/private balance in feminism. Women's documentary films were first produced primarily by and for younger feminists rooted in the New Left. The ideal type issue film emphasized the structures of women's oppression, and advocated collective solutions to women's prob-lems. In comparison with other feminist film genres, issue films presented a present-minded, rationalist analysis of women's lives. Women's docu-mentary films changed significantly from the issue films of the late 1960s to biographical and autobiographical portrait films of the mid-1970s. Typ-ically film portraits depict the private life of an individual woman strug-gling with quintessential female problems, reshaping her personal responses and interpersonal relationships from a feminist perspective (e.g. *Living With Peter; Not Together Now: End of a Marriage; Joyce at 34: Nana, Mom, and Me*). In so doing, film portraits offer their viewers models of and support for their own efforts at reshaping personal relationships.

Women's film portraits introduce new feminist heroes—strong women who have lived, or are changing, in accord with feminist values. The cinematic search for strong female predecessors is analogous to the ethnic search for roots insofar as it allows individual women to define themselves better by seeing how their particular life histories intersect with the col-lective historical experience of women.[3] Like the women's movement, portrait films explore ways in which particular women's identities are socially and historically structured. They embody both sides of the cen-tral feminist tension: by transcending public/private polarities women's film portraits represent a significant contribution to feminist art and ideology.

Women's avant-garde films and filmmakers reflect the most private, individualistic strains in feminism. Though excluded by New Leftists who initially defined and dominated the feminist film movement, many of them have been redefined as "feminist" and incorporated into the movement—

women's film festivals show them regularly, and more importantly, several women's cooperatives have formed to distribute avant-garde films.

In addition to producing films, feminist filmmakers created an alternative and relatively autonomous market in which their films are distributed and screened. In the early 1970s women filmmakers were excluded from existing distribution networks and were forced either to invent their own market or see their films die out for lack of an audience. As feminism gained legitimacy within schools, libraries, and other publicly funded institutions, it provided the financial and popular/political support crucial to the incipient film movement's growth and survival. Innovators made personal connections and invented marketing procedures which newcomers could then exploit, thus saving scarce time and money for other projects. Some early feminist filmmakers forged formal as well as informal cooperative networks which provided the basis for an ongoing feminist film movement. Feminist distribution cooperatives and feminist film festivals quickly developed into the core units of the new market. These core units solved the problematic marketing tasks for which they had been formed, but they served an equally important latent function of providing a supportive, relatively autonomous feminist milieu in which the filmmakers could work.

In producing and distributing their films with likeminded women, the filmmakers felt freer to develop the political dimensions and implications of their projects. The ongoing production of political culture goes against the grain of individual artistic expression and frequently must be nourished by a community of political artists and audiences. Suffragist filmmakers' efforts were supported by similar conditions. Working prior to the consolidation of the movie industry, pro-suffrage filmmakers also worked together to create political movies which presented their movement's goals to wider audiences. They collectively wrote, directed, and starred in the films, thus exhibiting cooperative creative control as extensive as that exercised by contemporary feminist filmmakers. Since Hollywood's consolidation in the hands of a few giant companies at the end of World War I, however, political filmmakers have been confined to "alternative" documentary filmmaking with very limited non-theatrical distribution.

Feminists, like other independent filmmakers, reached relatively small, specialized audiences which already shared many of their values and goals. The major segment of the feminist film audience consists of college students in women's studies and related courses. Women's film festivals are important showcases for the films, and feminist magazines and newspapers regularly review them. By creating an alternative market closely connected to the women's movement, feminist filmmakers and films have cemented their ties with the larger political movement from which they take intellectual and ideological sustenance. When shown in feminist settings, even the most personal portrait (and sometimes avant-garde) films are discussed in terms of their general relevance to women's lives. Far more than theatrical movies, feminist films have been part of an ongoing political/aesthetic dialog between filmmakers and their audiences. Consequently, the films' thematic and stylistic shifts have articulated closely with broader ideological and organizational shifts in the feminist movement. Until now the integrity of the feminist film movement has been part and parcel of the relative autonomy and intimacy of the feminist film world; women retained considerable control over the films they had created just as they maintained close contact with other feminist filmmakers and feminist audiences. Yet all of this may be changing.

Many feminist documentary filmmakers dream of, and for the first time some now face, the possibility of commercial success far beyond the bounds of the feminist film movement. If women succeed, as most of them want to, in making it in the theatrical movie market (writing and/or directing feature, fictionalized movies which are shown in regular movie theaters), the connections between feminism and film may strain or die out. Theatrical moviemaking bears little resemblance to the feminist film world: there are no significant support networks of women working in the mainstream industry, filmmakers do not retain control over the distribution and exhibition of their products, and film audiences are so large and diverse that they are not likely to share the filmmaker's political values. In addition, theatrical films are viewed as "entertainment" and are not accompanied by "consciousness-raising" discussions. Isolated from the ongoing politically-informed criticism of feminist coworkers and audiences, filmmakers may increasingly focus on the personal and neglect the political dimensions in women's lives. The public/private dualism central to contemporary feminism may be wholly absorbed into the overweaning individualism of American life. The shifting emphasis in Claudia Weill's work from *Joyce at 34,* a film which delicately balanced personal and political issues, to *Girlfriends,* a theatrical movie wholly concerned with private life and interpersonal relationships, may be prophetic.

In a more optimistic vein, however, feminist filmmakers may soon find themselves in a position to reach out effectively to the unconverted, and to broaden profoundly and expand discussions about women's lives, sex roles, personal identity, and the family. "Real movies," as *The Godfather* and *Norma Rae* have recently demonstrated, can set off serious discussions about the meaning and quality of our lives which reach far beyond the mostly female, 18-to-22-year-old college students who now constitute the overwhelming majority of feminist film viewers. For feminist filmmakers the problem will be to hold fast to a feminist vision in a world which has long been hostile to women. Women's support networks have developed in other arenas dominated by males (e.g. advertising and academia), and women "making it" in Hollywood may develop similar networks in their attempts to transform, rather than be transformed by, the Hollywood Dream Machine.

Methodological Appendix

Exemplary vs. Typical Respondents

In any complex sociological investigation certain problems of data acquisition and analysis confront the researcher. In this study data was gathered through in-depth interviews and participant observation,
supplemented by published materials. Respondents were selected according to their position in different sectors of the feminist film movement: documentarists and avant-gardists were included in proportion to
their total numbers in the population, as were women of different ages,
and those from different geographic regions. Although respondents were
selected according to their positions, personal differences in tempera-
ment, intelligence, and verbal skills meant that some of them were far
more articulate and insightful than others. Once the interviews were
underway the respondents fell into two ranked categories: those *exemplary* respondents who knew and communicated a great deal about the
workings of the feminist film movement and the *typical* respondents whose
knowledge was much more limited and closely tied to their narrower
personal experiences. My own involvement in the feminist film movement
as a distributor, conference organizer, screening committee member, and
critic generated certain hunches and insights which the respondents I
interviewed confirmed or refuted. Exemplary respondents were able to
frame and dramatize the issues, and to sum up the central tendencies of
the feminist film movement as corroborated by other sources, e.g. distributors, critics, and festival organizers. Because of this, their remarks
and observations reappear frequently throughout this study. Typical respondents blended into the whole, but their interviews do not include
incisive remarks about the feminist film movement; although they were
an important part of this study and of the sample population, they were
rarely quoted or directly referred to on the preceding pages.

The Problem of Money

The issue which proved most difficult to investigate was the financial basis
of the feminist film movement. For a variety of reasons, filmmakers, dis-

tributors, and festival organizers were unwilling (and sometimes unable) to provide specific, detailed information on film production costs and yearly sales and rental income. First, independent films are produced with borrowed equipment and donated labor. Skilled filmmakers work for free on their friends' films, and are repaid in kind. Better-equipped filmmakers may lend their cameras, tape recorders, or editing machines to others; processing companies often contribute raw film stock to a filmmaker. None of this shows up in a budget, of course.

Additional considerations prevented me from eliciting specific financial information on particular films. Perhaps the simplest explanation is that most Americans consider their income to be a very private, personal matter. In addition, artistic reputation is a delicate construction, held together in large part by the perceived market value of the artist. Since typical feminist filmmakers make so little money through film rentals and sales, they may hope to protect their reputations by withholding basic economic facts. Finally, financial data have direct financial implications for one's tax reports, and many filmmakers do not wish to have their financial status investigated or disclosed for this reason. Consequently, it was far easier to acquire aggregated financial data about several films by different filmmakers than it was to acquire disaggregated information on a specific film or on a particular filmmaker's entire oeuvre. Several recently published reports (Feinstein, ed., *The Independent Film Community* and Rothschild and Reichert, *Doing It Yourself*), for example, disclosed the annual gross income of New Day and also of some nonfeminist independent film distributors, thus enabling me to estimate relevant economic figures.

Appendix A

Sample of Filmmakers, by Age and Film Type

Older Documentarists

Madeline Anderson
Liane Brandon
Joyce Chopra
Nell Cox

Older Avant-Gardists

Connie Beeson
Storm de Hirsch
Amy Greenfield
Maria Lassnig
Gunvor Nelson
Carolee Schneeman
Rosalind Schneider

Younger Documentarists

Geri Ashur
Mirra Bank
Martha Coolidge
Judith Dancoff
Donna Deitch
Nancy Dowd
Mary Feldhaus-Weber
Jill Godmilow
Susan Kleckner
Margaret Lazarus
Jan Oxenberg

Julia Reichert
Amalie Rothschild
Judy Smith
Miriam Weinstein

Younger Avant-Gardists

Freude Bartlett
Suzanne Baumann
Jill Hultin

Younger Mixed Films

Lois Tupper

Appendix B

Audience Questionnaire

This questionnaire is part of a study of films by women and about women. I hope that you'll take the few minutes necessary to fill it out.

If you have seen films like this before, when did you first see it (or them)? Check one.

_____ 1975
_____ 1972-4
_____ before 1972
Please name some of them.

How often have you seen films like this before today? Check one answer.

_____ this is my first
_____ one or two others
_____ between three and ten others
_____ more than ten

How did you hear about this film showing? (Check as many as apply).

_____ daily newspaper or radio
_____ women's studies course or program
_____ friend
_____ women's center or women's publication
_____ film course or program
_____ women's consciousness-raising group
_____ other (please write a brief explanation)

What do you like most about these films? Mention as many things as you wish.

What do you dislike most about these films? Again, mention whatever you wish.

How often do you usually see movies at any of the following places? The choices are:

A more than once a week
B once every week or two
C once every three or four weeks
D less than once a month
E never

Please circle the appropriate letter after each of the following:

regular movie theater   A   B   C   D   E
television   A   B   C   D   E
women's center   A   B   C   D   E
museum   A   B   C   D   E
classroom   A   B   C   D   E
other (please explain briefly)

Please check any of the words listed below which closely describe your relationship to the movies.

_____ fan
_____ critic
_____ filmmaker or aspiring filmmaker
_____ feminist
_____ occasional viewer
_____ other (a brief explanation, please)

How many feminist books have you read in the last year?

_____ none
_____ 1-2
_____ 3-8
_____ more than 8

Do you agree or disagree with the following statements? (Check one for each statement).

Agree	*Disagree*	
_____	_____	Feminist organizations should include only women.
_____	_____	Women who picket and participate in protests are setting a bad example for children.
_____	_____	Women are right to be unhappy with their role in American society but wrong in the way they're protesting.

____	____	The relationship of a woman to another woman is as important as a woman's relationship to a man.
____	____	A woman has a right to put her own fulfillment above that of her husband and children.
____	____	True feminists should not be married.

Please state how many, if any, of the following women's organizations you belong to.

number

national organizations (like N.O.W., W.E.A.L.) _____
professional organizations _____
local women's centers and organizations _____
consciousness-raising groups _____
other (please name and briefly describe them) _____

How old are you _____ Check if you are female _____ or male _____ .
What is your occupation? _____

Thank you for participating in this study. Please leave the questionnaire with me before you leave.

JAN ROSENBERG

Notes

Chapter 1

1. See Betty Friedan, *The Feminine Mystique* (New York: Norton, 1963), for the earliest statement of this position.

2. Peter Feinstein, ed., *The Independent Film Community; A Report on the Status of Independent Film in the United States* (New York: Committee on Film and Television Resources and Services, 1977), p. 2.

3. The most important exceptions to date are *Hester Street* and *Girlfriends*, both of which have enjoyed successful theatrical runs in selected cities.

4. Enormous problems confront researchers who attempt to investigate these early films. Most of them have actually disintegrated, and those which have managed to survive are not adequately catalogued.

5. Quoted in Marjorie Rosen, *Popcorn Venus; Women, Movies, and the American Dream* (New York: Coward, McCann, and Geohagan, 1973), p. 33.

6. Ibid.

7. Jane Addams, *The Second Twenty Years at Hull House* (New York: Macmillan, 1930), p. 375. "The release function of art, the offering of an escape from the monotony of daily living is doubtless provided most widely by the movie and its new child the talkee. . . . [audiences] all come with a simple desire to be amused or a willingness to be instructed if done entertainingly."

8. Robert Sklar, *Movie-Made America* (New York: Random House, 1975), p. 141.

9. William Nichols, untitled article in *Screen,* Vol. 13, No. 4 (1972-73), p. 108.

10. Lewis Jacobs, *The Rise of the American Film; A Critical History* (New York: Teachers College Press, 1968).

11. See Stewart Ewen, *Captains of Consciousness: Advertising and the Social Roots of the Consumer Culture* (New York: McGraw Hill, 1976), for a social history of the advertising industry in the twentieth century. Advertising is a major branch of the consciousness industry and provides an interesting point of comparison.

12. See *Film Culture*, No. 50-51 (Fall & Winter 1970), special issue on Hollywood Blacklisting, for discussion of McCarthyism in Hollywood.

13. Juliet Mitchell, *Woman's Estate* (New York: Pantheon, 1971). Mitchell was one of the first feminist theorists to integrate personal life into her theoretical formulations.

14. Leif Furhammer and Folke Isaksson, *Politics and Film* (New York: Praeger, 1973).

15. Jack Morrison, *The Rise of the Arts on the American Campus* (New York: McGraw-Hill, 1973), especially p. 16.

16. Peter Cowie, *A Concise History of the Cinema* (New York: A. S. Barnes and Co., 1971), Vol. 2, p. 238.

Chapter 2

1. Feminists' early and continuing focus on media was apparent from the founding of NOW, at which time Muriel Fox headed a national task force on Women and the Media, to the Resolution on Women and Media passed in 1977 at the National Women's Conference in Houston. In addition, several of the now classic feminist anthologies and texts include sections on women and media, further reflecting and reinforcing feminists' media concerns. See Betty Friedan, *The Feminine Mystique* (New York: Norton, 1973); Robin Morgan, ed., *Sisterhood is Powerful* (New York: Random House, 1970); Judith Hole and Ellen Levine, *Rebirth of Feminism* (New York: Quadrangle Books, 1971); and Gornick and Moran, *Women in Sexist Society* (New York: Basic Books, 1971).

2. Jo Freeman, "The Origins of the Women's Movement," *American Journal of Sociology,* Vol. 78, No. 4 (1973). Maren Lockwood Carden, *The New Feminist Movement* (New York: Russell Sage, 1973).

3. Freeman, "Origins of the Women's Movement," p. 799.

4. Jo Freeman, "Women on the Move: the Roots of Revolt," in Alice Rossi and Ann Calderwood, eds. *Academic Women on the Move* (New York: Russell Sage, 1973), pp. 15-16.

5. Harmony Hammond, "Feminist Abstract Art—A Political Viewpoint," *Heresies,* Vol. 1, No. 1 (1977).

6. Interview with Rosalind Schneider, August 1975.

7. Quoted in Betty Friedan, *It Changed My Life* (New York: Random House, 1976), p. 87.

8. Betty Friedan's landmark book was based on years of intimate work within the media and involves some mea culpa.

9. Midge Kovacs, *New York Times,* Aug. 26, 1972; quoted in *Media Report to Women,* Sept. 29, 1972, p. 3.

10. Friedan, *It Changed My Life,* p. 95.

11. Interview with Midge Kovacs, April 1976.

12. Interview with Kristina Nordstrom, August 1975.

13. Quoted in *Media Report to Women,* Sept. 29, 1972, p. 4.

14. *Variety,* Dec. 10, 1975, p. 1.

15. Interview with Donna Allen, January 1977.

16. Nine films in my sample were completed in 1971. They are: *Growing Up Female: As Six Become One, The Woman's Film, Janie's Janie, Three Lives, Anything You Want to Be, Sisters, Make Out, Genesis 3:16, It Happens to Us.*

17. It seems likely that between 25 and 35 feminist films were produced in 1975 and 1976.

The rate of growth definitely slowed because many filmmakers, especially those whose reputations were established, undertook larger, more expensive film projects which took longer to launch and to complete. Of the 20 documentary filmmakers in my sample, for instance, at least 8 were at work on some major aspect of a feature film or series for television or movie theaters. These are: Mirra Bank, Joyce Chopra, Martha Coolidge, Nell Cox, Mary Feldhaus-Weber, Jill Godmilow, Julia Reichert, and Miriam Weinstein.

18. My discussions with feminist filmmakers and film critics from France, Germany, England, and Canada form the basis of my views.

19. Robert Kramer, "Newsreel," in John Stuart Katz, ed., *Perspectives on the Study of Film* (Boston: Little, Brown, 1971), pp. 237-38.

20. Jack Morrison, *The Rise of the Arts on the American Campus* (New York: McGraw-Hill, 1973).

21. Carden, *New Feminist Movement,* p. 65.

22. Most of these are listed in three directories of the feminist film movement: Bonnie Dawson, *Women's Films in Print* (San Francisco: Booklegger Press, 1975); Jeanne Betancourt, *Women in Focus* (Dayton, Ohio: Pflaum Publishing, 1974); Sharon Smith, *Women Who Make Movies* (New York: Hopkinson and Blake, 1975).

23. Jo Freeman, "The Tyranny of Structurelessness," *Berkeley Journal of Sociology.*

24. In addition to Freeman, "Origins of the Women's Movement," and Carden, *New Feminist Movement,* see Juliet Mitchell, *Women's Estate* (New York: Pantheon, 1971).

25. Newsreel did not actually distribute *Janie's Janie;* it was a victim of then ascendent "Third Worldism" within N.Y. Newsreel. But former Newsreel members formed a radical film distribution company, *Odeon,* which incorporated values, skills, and contacts that had developed in Newsreel. Odeon distributed *Janie's Janie* from the outset.

26. The third film, *Make Out,* was conceived more as an "exercise" for inexperienced women filmmakers than as a financially or even politically viable project. The film dramatized the sexual subordination and exploitation of teenaged girls. Unlike other Newsreel films, it did not connect this with larger political or economic structures of inequality.

27. Interview with Judy Smith, January 1976.

28. This lends support to William Nichols' observation that Newsreel acted as a "barometer" rather than as a vanguard of the New Left. See William James Nichols, *Newsreel, Film and Revolution* (M.A. thesis, U.C.L.A., 1972), p. 51.

29. Carden, *Feminism in 1975: The Non-Establishment, the Establishment, and the Future* (New York: Ford Foundation, 1976).

30. Ibid., p. 21.

31. See Alice Rossi, "Feminism and Intellectual Complexity," in Alice Rossi, ed., *The Feminist Papers* (New York: Bantam, 1974), for a suggestive discussion of the dialectic between personal and political feminist orientations.

32. *The Feminist Art Journal,* Vol. 4, No. 2 (Summer 1975), p. 4.

33. Patricia Erens, "Making and Distributing *Nana, Mom and Me,*" *The Feminist Art Journal,* Vol. 4, No. 2 (Summer 1975), p. 13.

34. In *Of Woman Born*, Adrienne Rich continually hearkens back to the importance that becoming a mother has on a woman's relationship to her own mother. She writes, "The experience of giving birth stirs deep reverberations of her mother in a daughter; women often dream of their mothers during pregnancy and labor" (p. 220). In another passage Rich suggests the broader ramifications which motherhood holds for the mother-daughter relationship. "For those of us who had children, and later came to recognize and act upon the breadth and depth of our feelings for women, a complex new bond with our mothers is possible" (p. 232).

35. Christopher Lasch, "The Narcissist Society," *New York Review of Books,* Sept. 30, 1976, pp. 5-13; Richard Sennett, "Destructive Gemeinschaft," *Partisan Review,* 3 (1976), pp. 341-61; Richard Kazis, "Berger-Tanner and the New Narcissism," *Socialist Revolution,* Vol. 7, No. 5.

36. Erens, p. 16.

37. Molly Haskell, "Time to Judge Women's Films on Merit," *Village Voice,* Dec. 29, 1975, p. 68.

Chapter 3

1. Everett C. Hughes, *Men and Their Work* (New York: Free Press, 1958); Sara Rudick and Pamela Daniels, *Working It Out* (New York: Pantheon, 1977).

2. P. Adams Sitney, *Visionary Film; the American Avant Garde* (New York: Oxford University Press, 1974); Sheldon Renan, *An Introduction to the American Underground Film* (New York: Dutton, 1967).

3. Bonnie Dawson, *Women's Films in Print* (San Francisco: Booklegger Press, 1975); Jeanne Betancourt, *Women in Focus* (Dayton, Ohio: Pflaum Publishing, 1974); Sharon Smith, *Women Who Make Movies* (New York: Hopkinson and Blake, 1975).

4. All film movement members I spoke to agreed that documentarists dominated the feminist film movement from the start. Their films are still the best known, they established and run the core support systems, and they have achieved more prominence than avant-garde filmmakers. The 2 to 1 ratio is my rough numerical translation of the relative importance of the two groups.

5. Typical examples of the father's occupations from which the occupational status categories were developed are: *upper middle class:* doctor, lawyer, banker; *middle middle class:* teacher, social worker, small businessman; *lower middle class:* policeman, secretary (in female-headed family).

6. Cesar Graña, *Bohemian Versus Bourgeois; French Society and the French Man of Letters in the Nineteenth Century* (New York: Basic Books, 1964), p. 23; Bernard Rosenberg and Norris Fliegel, *The Vanguard Artist* (Chicago: Quadrangle, 1965), pp. 122-25.

7. Professional quality 16 millimeter cameras, for example, cost upwards of $4,000, and synchronized tape recorders cost another $2,000 to $3,000. Editing tables cost more than $20,000.

8. Mason Griff, "The Recruitment of the Artist," in R.N. Wilson, ed., *The Arts in Society* (Englewood Cliffs, N.J.: Prentice-Hall, 1964), p. 85.

9. Interview with Jan Oxenberg, August 1975.

10. Judy Chicago and Mirian Schapiro had just begun a very dynamic feminist arts programs at California Institute of the Arts when Oxenberg entered there as a graduate student, and filmmaking was an integral part of that program.

11. Interview with Jan Oxenberg, August 1975.

12. Interview with Judy Smith, November 1975.

13. Interview with Lois Tupper, January 1976.

14. Richard Schickel, "The Movies Are Now High Art," in David Manning White, ed., *Pop Culture in America* (Chicago: Quadrangle, 1969), pp. 141-52.

15. Herbert Gans, *Popular Culture and High Culture* (New York: Basic Books, 1974), pp. 81-85.

16. Interview with Martha Coolidge, October 1975.

17. Interview with Geri Ashur, September 1975.

18. Cinéma vérité was a very influential documentary film movement in the late 1950s and 1960s which popularized the use of lightweight cameras and recording equipment in its search for *authenticity*. Like traditional documentaries, cinéma vérité films dealt with ". . . fact rather than fiction, with real places, people, and events rather than imagined ones." Louis D. Giannetti, *Understanding Movies* (Englewood Cliffs, N.J.: Prentice-Hall, 1972), p. 192. Further defining characteristics of cinéma véité, compared to traditional documentaries, are the avoidance of the use of narration, of professional actors, of artificial lighting, and even a prohibition against restaging or reenacting actual events.

19. Interview with Geri Ashur, September 1975.

20. Interview with Suzanne Baumann, September 1975.

21. Interview with Amy Greenfield, October 1975.

22. Everett C. Hughes, *The Sociological Eye* (Chicago: Aldine, 1971), p. 295.

23. Sheldon Renan, *An Introduction to the American Underground Film* (New York: Dutton, 1967), p. 17.

24. Interview with Nell Cox, November 1975.

25. Interview with Joyce Chopra, January 1976.

26. Stephen Mamber, "Direct Cinema and the Crisis Structure," *Screen*, Vol. 13, No. 3 (Autumn 1972), p. 116.

27. Interview with Connie Beeson, November 1975.

28. Martin K.E. Green, "Interview with Storm de Hirsch," in *Super-8 Filmmaker*, Vol. 2, No. 1 (Jan.- Feb. 1974), p. 29.

29. Interview with Amy Greenfield, October 1975.

30. Interview with Gunvor Nelson, November 1975.

31. Ibid.

32. "A Conversation—Shirley Clarke and Storm de Hirsch," *Film Culture*, 46 (Autumn 1968), p. 51.

33. Interview with Gunvor Nelson, November 1975.

34. Interview with Rosalind Schneider, August 1975.

35. Rosalind Schneider, Forum on Women's Art, Brooklyn, New York, March 1974.

36. Letter to Jeanne Betancourt.

37. This and the following two quotations by Julia Reichert are taken from Betancourt, *Women in Focus,* p. 69.

38. Interview with Judy Smith, November 1975.

39. Interview with Mirra Bank, October 1978.

40. Interview with Joyce Chopra, January 1976.

41. Interview with Geri Ashur, September 1975.

42. Interview with Nell Cox, November 1975.

Chapter 4

1. Ruth McCormick, "Women's Liberation Cinema," *Cineaste,* Vol. 5, No. 2 (Spring 1972), p. 7

2. Karl Mannheim, "The Utopian Mentality," in *Ideology and Utopia* (New York: Harcourt, Brace, and World, Inc.: 1936).

3. Max Weber, *The Theory of Social and Economic Organization* (New York: Oxford University Press, 1947), p. 272.

4. Christopher Lasch, "The Narcissist Society," *New York Review of Books,* Sept. 30, 1976; Richard Sennett, "Destructive Gemeinschaft," *Partisan Review,* 3 (1976); Tom Wolfe, "The 'Me' Decade and the Third Great Awakening," *New York Magazine,* 9 (Aug. 23, 1976).

5. Richard Kazis, "Berger-Tanner and the 'New Narcissism,' " *Socialist Revolution,* Vol. 7, No. 5 (1977), p. 145.

6. Betty Friedan, "An Open Letter to the Women's Movement," *It Changed My Life* (New York: Random House, 1976), pp. 369-70.

7. Alice Rossi, "Contemporary American Feminism: In and Out of the Political Mainstream," paper delivered to an International Symposium on Research on Popular Movements, Stockholm, Sweden, Feb. 7, 1978.

8. Alice Rossi, "Sex is a Many Sided Thing," in Alice Rossi, ed., *The Feminist Papers* (New York: Bantam, 1974); Alice Rossi, "Contemporary American Feminism: In and Out of the Political Mainstream," unpublished paper. Also see Richard Gambino, *Blood of My Blood* (New York: Doubleday, 1974), for an interesting discussion of alternating generational commitment to Italian core values among Italian-American ethnics. According to Gambino, "The culture of the old country had to be screened by the second generation, the first that had the formidable challenge of establishing a native-born American identity. But the elements of Italian culture which were screened out may prove to be an asset to the third and fourth generations," (p. 145).

9. Betty Friedan, "Cooking with Betty Friedan . . . Yes. Betty Friedan," *New York Times,* Jan. 5, 1977, pp. 49-50.

10. Sara Ruddick and Pamela Daniels, *Working It Out* (New York: Pantheon, 1977).

11. Three major guidebooks to the feminist film movement were published in 1974-75; these will be discussed in the next chapter on institutionalization.

12. In discussions with filmmaker Madeline Anderson I learned that both audience types constitute major segments of the film's market.

13. In formal and technical terms, it is more skillfully constructed and tightly conceived than many other feminist films; its maker, Madeline Anderson, was an experienced film editor and producer before she made this film. Unlike many feminist filmmakers who began making documentary films in order to communicate their political ideas, without any prior knowledge of filmmaking, Anderson was an experienced professional film-maker who started out in cinéma vérité.

14. Interview with Connie Beeson, November 1975.

15. Interview with Kristina Nordstrom, August 1975.

16. Ingmar Bergman's *Persona* plays off a similar contrast. In the scene in which the nurse carefully describes her sexual encounters on the beach, her voice remains calm and her face seems completely unemotional. *Betty Tells Her Story* makes this contrast one of its themes.

17. Whitney Museum Program Notes, Dec. 17-27, 1975.

18. Cambridge Documentary Films Catalog, no date, no page number.

19. Sylvia Gillet, "A Free Reeling Feminist: Interview with Julia Reichert," *Women; a Journal of Liberation,* Vol. 3, No. 2 (1973), p. 10. [emphasis mine]

20. Mannheim, p. 235.

21. Ibid.

22. The following passage from William Butler Yeats expresses these views for some—*if* one could change the pronoun to "she":
". . . guard me from those thoughts men think
In the mind alone.
He that sings a lasting song
thinks in the marrow bone."

23. Interview with Mirra Bank, July 1976.

24. Gerda Lerner, "Doing Women's History," *Journal of Interdisciplinary History.*

25. Interview with Martha Coolidge, September 1975. [emphasis mine]

26. Kazis, p. 145.

27. C. Wright Mills, *The Sociological Imagination* (New York: Oxford University Press, 1959).

28. cf. Nancy Chodorow, *The Reproduction of Mothering: Psychoanalysis and the Sociology of Gender* (Berkeley: University of California Press, 1978).

29. Max Weber, *The Theory of Social and Economic Organization* (New York: Oxford University Press, 1947), p. 41. [emphasis mine]

30. Ibid., p. 95.

31. cf. Herbert Gans, *Popular and High Culture* (New York: Basic Books, 1974).

32. Serious Business Catalog, no date, p. 32.

33. Amos Vogel, quoted in Serious Business Catalog, no date, p. 125.

34. "Interview with Gunvor Nelson," *Canyon Cinema News,* No. 3 (May-June 1974), pp. 6-7.

35. Harold Rosenberg, *The Tradition of the New* (New York: McGraw-Hill, 1965).

36. "Storm de Hirsch, Independent Filmmaker," *Super 8 Filmmaker,* Vol. 2, No. 1 (Jan.-Feb. 1974), p. 26.

37. Gans, p. 77.

38. "Poetry in the Film: A Symposium," in P. Adams Sitney, ed., *Film Culture Reader* (New York: Praeger, 1970), pp. 173-74.

39. "A Conversation—Shirley Clarke and Storm de Hirsch," *Film Culture*, No. 46 (Autumn 1968).

40. Paul Johnson, *Enemies of Society* (New York: Atheneum, 1977), pp. 32ff.

41. As in the previous categorization, three raters evaluated these films. They were presented with a list of major themes, and asked to indicate one central theme for each film. There was basic agreement among the raters: all three raters agreed in 51 cases (68 percent complete agreement), two agreed in 12 cases (16 percent), and there was no agreement among the raters in the remaining 12 cases.

42. Camille Cook, quoted in Serious Business Catalog, no date, p. 13.

Chapter 5

1. Howard Becker, "Art as Collective Action," *American Sociological Review,* Vol. 39, No. 6 (1974), p. 769.

2. Robert Sklar, *Movie-Made America* (New York: Random House, 1975).

3. Richard Christopherson, "Making Art with Machines: Photographies Institutional Inadequacies," *Urban Life and Culture,* Vol. 3, No. 1 (1974).

4. Private foundations exhibit the same basis in favor of documentary over avant-garde films.

5. The Filmmakers' Coop is not legally a non-profit corporation, but it does not actually make profits and does not exist in order to make profits. Individual filmmakers, not the coop per se, earn the profits.

6. Data based on interview with Eric Breitbart, October 1978.

7. Peter Feinstein, ed., *The Independent Film Community; a Report on the Status of Independent Film in the United States* (New York: Committee on Film and Television Resources and Services, 1977), pp. 30-32.

8. Julia Reichert and Amalie Rothschild, *Doing It Yourself* (New York: Association of Independent Video and Filmmakers, 1977), p. 42.

9. Feinstein, pp. 37-38.

10. *Cinéaste* and *Jump Cut* are the most important political film magazines in America, and both regularly review documentary films.

11. P. Adams Sitney, *Visionary Film; the American Avant Garde* (New York: Oxford University Press, 1974), p. ix.

12. The American emphasis on experience before and distinct from theory is institutionalized in film schools, which separate the two types of study—film production and film criticism.

13. Some films were already being distributed. Newsreel had its own distribution network for the films which it produced. Kate Millett found a distributor for *Three Lives* on the basis of her reputation as a best-selling feminist author.

14. Women/Artist/Filmmakers was formed as much to consolidate fundraising efforts of the members, who were out-distanced by the better-organized documentarists, as to promote their distribution.

15. New Day Films, Catalog, 1976, no page numbers.

16. Frances Reid, "Iris Films: Documenting the Lives of Lesbians," *Heresies, A Feminist Publication on Art and Politics,* Fall 1977, p. 100.

17. Ibid., p. 100.

18. Women's Film Coop Catalog, no date, p. 4.

19. Julia Reichert and Jim Klein had formed New Day in the spring of 1971, to distribute their first film, *Growing Up Female: As Six Become One.* But the excitement generated about feminist documentaries at the Flaherty Film Seminar that summer had important ramifications for New Day. Amalie Rothschild, another feminist documentarist, joined New Day, and within a couple of months Liane Brandon also became a member of New Day.

20. The first three films were *Growing Up Female: As Six Become One, It Happens to Us,* and *Anything You Want to Be.*

21. Diana Crane, *Invisible Colleges; Diffusion of Knowledge in Scientific Communities* (Chicago: University of Chicago Press, 1972).

22. New Day Films Catalog, no date, p. 5.

23. Women's Film Coop Catalog, 1973, p. 2; [emphasis mine].

24. Additional differences further separate the Women's Film Coop from New Day. On joining New Day a filmmaker must pay about $3,000 towards advertising and mailing costs, while filmmakers whose films are picked up by the Women's Film Coop do not pay anything. In addition, in New Day incomes from film sales and rentals go directly to the films' creators, while the Women's Film Coop uses revenues from all films to cover costs of operating the Coop. Thus, successful films in the Women's Film Coop subsidize the others. Though the Women's Film Coop was supposed to pay royalties to the filmmakers based on their film's revenues, the operating expenses continually depleted the Coop's income.

25. Interview with Freude Bartlett, November 1975.

26. Serious Business Company Catalog, no date, p. 26.

27. Reichert and Rothschild.

28. Several years later Rosalind Schneider, the organizer of the New York Cultural Center women's film program, was instrumental in founding Women / Artist / Filmmakers.

29. Typical rental price structure is: lowest fee is for one "closed" educational booking, usually about one dollar per minute; more "closed" educational screenings cost the rentor more money; paid entry, "open" screenings are the most expensive.

30. Hans Magnus Enzenberger, *The Consciousness Industry; on Literature, Politics and the Media* (New York: Seabury Press, 1974).

31. Interview with Christina Nordstrom, August 1975.

32. Quoted in Jonas Mekas, "Movie Journal," *Village Voice,* June 1, 1972, p. 28.

33. Feature films directed by women, like industrial and most animation films, are not counted as part of the independent feminist film movement.

34. Joan Braderman, untitled article, *Artforum,* Vol. 11, No. 1, p. 87.

35. The Association of American Colleges condensed the Festival I program notes and mailed them to thousands of people who requested them.

36. Molly Haskell, "Women Under the Influence of Film: Is This Women's Film Festival Necessary?", *Village Voice,* Sept. 20, 1976, p. 91.

37. I spoke to the following filmmaker/distributors about this: Freude Bartlett of Serious Business Company, Joyce Chopra and Mirra Bank from New Day, Eric Breitbart from Odeon, and Rosalind Schneider from Women / Artist / Filmmakers.

38. As several respondents noted in their questionnaires, the question "How often have you seen films like this before?" is very vague. Does "like this" mean independent films, feminist documentaries, feminist avant-garde films, or something else? The question was purposely vague to accommodate all types of films.

39. Much of this discussion parallels, and is indebted to, Richard Christopherson's analysis of photography. See Christopherson, ibid., for the development of his views.

40. Jeanne Betancourt, *Women in Focus* (Dayton, Ohio: Pflaum Publishing, 1974); Bonnie Dawson, *Women's Films in Print* (San Francisco: Booklegger Press, 1975); Sharon Smith, *Women Who Make Movies* (New York: Hopkinson and Blake, 1975).

41. Betancourt, p. vi.

42. William James Nichols, *Newsreel, Film and Revolution* (Master's thesis, U.C.L.A., 1972), p. 51.

43. Molly Haskell, "Time to Judge Women's Films on Merit," *Village Voice,* Dec. 29, 1975, p. 68.

44. Claire Johnston, "Women's Cinema as Counter-Cinema," in Claire Johnston, ed., *Notes on Women's Cinema* (London: Society for Education in Film and Television, n.d.).

45. E. Ann Kaplan, "Feminist Cinema: Contradiction or Consummation? A Discussion of Mulvey and Wollen's Riddles of the Sphinx," unpublished paper.

46. Alice Rossi's pioneering essay, "A Biosocial Perspective on Parenting," forced intellectual feminists to ask some questions which had been taboo about *biological* underpinnings of sex roles. Nancy Chodorow, working in a somewhat different direction, has also been exploring the sources of gender-linked psychic structures.

47. Lucy Lippard implicitly and explicitly addresses these issues throughout her recent work. See her *From the Center: Feminist Essays on Women's Art* (New York: E.P. Dutton and Company, 1976), especially the essay "The Women Artists' Movement—What Next?", pp. 139-48.

48. Unless otherwise indicated, all remarks by Mirra Bank in this section were made during an interview in September 1978.

49. Although Bank did one cooperative mailing, with two similar films, to a list of Jewish community groups, she never made any serious, systematic effort to exploit the special markets.

Chapter 6

1. Virginia Woolf immediately comes to mind as an "earlier" feminist who placed primary emphasis on the private sphere. See Alice Rossi, "Guineas and Locks: Virginia Woolf (1882-1941)," in Alice Rossi, ed., *The Feminist Papers* (New York: Bantam, 1974), pp. 622-26.

2. Mary Jo Buhle, "Intellectual Feminism of the 1910s." Revised unpublished paper, 1975.

3. Tamara K. Hareven, "The Search for Generational Memory: Tribal Rites in Industrial Society," *Daedalus,* Vol. 107, No. 4 (1978), pp. 137-49.

Bibliography

Addams, Jane. *The Second Twenty Years at Hull House.* New York: Macmillan, 1930.

Becker, Howard. "Art as Collective Action." *American Sociological Review,* Vol. 39, No. 6 (1974), pp. 767-76.

Betancourt, Jeanne. *Women in Focus.* Dayton, Ohio: Pflaum Publishing, 1974.

Braderman, Joan. Untitled article. *Artforum,* Vol. 11, No. 1 (1972).

Carden, Maren Lockwood. *Feminism in 1975: the Non-Establishment, the Establishment, and the Future.* New York: Ford Foundation, 1976.

_____. *The New Feminist Movement.* New York: Russell Sage, 1974.

Castro, Davis, and Stoll, Jerry. "Profile of Art in Revolution." In John Stuart Katz, ed., *Perspectives on the Study of the Film,* pp. 248-53.

Chodorow, Nancy. "Family Structure and Feminine Personality." In Michelle Z. Rosaldo and Louise Lamphere, eds., *Woman, Culture, and Society* (Stanford: Stanford University, 1974).

_____. *The Reproduction of Mothering: Psychoanalysis and the Sociology of Gender* (Berkeley: University of California Press, 1978).

Christopherson, Richard. "Making Art with Machines: Photography's Institutional Inadequacies." *Urban Life and Culture,* Vol. 3, No. 1 (1974), pp. 3-34.

"A Conversation—Shirley Clarke and Storm de Hirsch." *Film Culture,* Vol. 46 (Autumn 1968).

Coser, Lewis. "Publishers as Gatekeepers of Ideas." *Annals of the American Academy of Political Science,* Vol. 421 (Sept. 1975), pp. 14-22.

Cowie, Peter. *A Concise History of the Cinema.* New York: A.S. Barnes and Co., 1971.

Crane, Diana. *Invisible Colleges; Diffusion of Knowledge in Scientific Communities.* Chicago: University of Chicago Press, 1972.

Dawson, Bonnie. *Women's Films in Print.* San Francisco: Booklegger Press, 1975.

Enzenberger, Hans Magnus. *The Consciousness Industry; on Literature, Politics and the Media.* New York: Seabury Press, 1974.

Erens, Patricia. "Making and Distributing *Nana, Mom, and Me.*" *The Feminist Art Journal,* Summer 1975.

Ewen, Stewart. *Captains of Consciousness: Advertising and the Social Roots of the Consumer Culture.* New York: McGraw-Hill, 1976.

Feinstein, Peter, ed. *The Independent Film Community; a Report on the Status of Independent Film in the United States.* New York: Committee on Film and Television Resources and Services, 1977.

Film Culture, 50-51. Special issue on Hollywood Blacklisting.

Films By and/or About Women. Berkeley: Women's History Research Center, 1972.

Freeman, Jo. "The Origins of the Women's Movement." *American Journal of Sociology,* Vol. 78, No. 4 (1973).

————. "The Tyranny of Structurelessness." *Ms.*, Vol. 2, No. 1 (July 1973).

————. "Women on the Move: the Roots of Revolt." In Rossi and Calderwood, eds. *Academic Women on the Move.* New York: Russell Sage, 1973, pp. 15-16.

Friedan, Betty. "Cooking with Betty Friedan . . . Yes. Betty Friedan." *New York Times,* Jan. 5, 1977, pp. 49-50.

————. *The Feminine Mystique.* New York: Norton, 1963.

————. *It Changed My Life.* New York: Random House, 1976.

Furhammer, Leif, and Isaksson, Folke. *Politics and Film.* New York: Praeger, 1971.

Gambino, Richard. *Blood of My Blood.* New York: Doubleday, 1974.

Gans, Herbert. *Popular Culture and High Culture.* New York: Basic Books, 1974.

Gianetti, Louis D. *Understanding Movies.* Englewood Cliffs, N.J.: Prentice Hall, 1972.

Gillett, Sylvia. "A Free Reeling Feminist: Interview with Julia Reichert." *Women, A Journal of Liberation,* Vol. 3, No. 2.

Gornick, Vivian, and Moran, Barbara K., eds. *Women in Sexist Society.* New York: Basic Books, 1971.

Graña, César. *Bohemian versus Bourgeois; French Society and the French Man of Letters in the Nineteenth Century.* New York: Basic Books, 1964.

Green, Martyn K.E. "Interview with Storm de Hirsch." *Super-8 Filmmaker,* Vol. 2, No. 1 (1974).

Griff, Mason, "The Recruitment of the Artist." In R.N. Wilson, ed., *The Arts in Society.* Englewood Cliffs, N.J.: Prentice-Hall, 1964.

Hammond, Harmony. "Feminist Abstract Art—A Political Viewpoint." *Heresies: A Feminist Publication on Art,* Vol. 1, No. 1 (1977).

Haskell, Molly. *From Reverence to Rape; the Treatment of Women in the Movies.* New York: Holt, Rinehart and Winston, 1973.

————. "Time to Judge Women's Films on Merit." *Village Voice,* Dec. 29, 1975, p. 68.

————. "Women Under the Influence of Film: Is this Women's Film Festival Necessary?" *Village Voice,* Sept. 20, 1976.

Hole, Judith, and Levine, Ellen. *Rebirth of Feminism.* New York: Quadrangle Books, 1971.

Hughes, Everett C. *Men and Their Work.* New York: Free Press, 1958.

————. *The Sociological Eye.* Chicago: Aldine, 1971.

Jacobs, Lewis. *The Rise of the American Film; A Critical History.* New York: Teachers College Press, 1968.

Johnson, Paul. *Enemies of Society.* New York: Atheneum, 1977.

Johnston, Claire. "Women's Cinema as Counter-Cinema." In Johnston, Claire, ed. *Notes on Women's Cinema.* London: Society for Education in Film and Television, 1974.

Kaplan, E. Ann. "Feminist Cinema: Contradiction or Consummation? A Discussion of Mulvey and Wollen's Riddles of the Sphinx." Unpublished paper, 1978.

Katz, John Stuart, comp. *Perspectives on the Study of Film.* Boston: Little, Brown, 1971.

Kazis, Richard. "Berger-Tanner and the New Narcissim." *Socialist Revolution,* Vol. 7, No. 5 (1977).

Kramer, Robert. "Newsreel." In Stuart Katz, ed. *Perspectives on the Study of Film.* Boston: Little, Brown, 1971.

Lasch, Christopher. "The Narcissist Society." *New York Review of Books,* Sept. 30, 1976.

Lerner, Gerda. "New Approaches for the Study of Women in American History." *Journal of Social History,* Vol. 3, No. 1 (1969), pp. 53-62.

Lippard, Lucy. *From the Center; Feminist Essays on Women's Art.* New York: E.P. Dutton and Co., 1976.

Mamber, Stephen. "Direct Cinema and the Crisis Structure." *Screen,* Vol. 13, No. 3 (1972).

Mannheim, Karl. "The Utopian Mentality." In *Ideology and Utopia.* New York: Harcourt, Brace, and World, Inc., 1936.

McCormick, Ruth. "Women's Liberation Cinema." *Cinéaste,* Vol. 5, No. 2, p. 7.

Mellen, Joan. *Women and their Sexuality in the New Film.* New York: Horizon Press, 1973.

Mills, C. Wright. *The Sociological Imagination.* New York: Oxford University Press, 1959.

Mitchell, Juliet. *Women's Estate.* New York: Pantheon, 1971.

Morgan, Robin, ed. *Sisterhood is Powerful.* New York: Random House, 1970.

Morrison, Jack. *The Rise of the Arts on the American Campus.* New York: McGraw-Hill, 1973.

Nichols, William James. *Newsreel, Film and Revolution.* Master's thesis, U.C.L.A., 1972.

————. Untitled article. *Screen,* Vol. 13, No. 4 (1972-73).

Nin, Anais. *The Diary of Anais Nin.* New York: Swallow Press, 1966.

"Poetry and the Film: A Symposium." P. Adams Sitney, ed. *Film Culture Reader.* New York: Praeger, 1970.

Reichert, Julia, and Rothschild, Amalie. *Doing It Yourself.* New York: Association of Independent Video and Filmmakers, 1977.

Reid, Frances. "Iris Films: Documenting the Lives of Lesbians." *Heresies* (Fall 1977).

Renan, Sheldon. *An Introduction to the American Underground Film.* New York: Dutton, 1967.

Rich, Adrienne. *Of Woman Born; Motherhood as Experience and Institution.* New York: Norton, 1976.

Rosen, Marjorie. *Popcorn Venus; Women, Movies, and the American Dream.* New York: Coward, McCann, and Geohagan, 1973.

Rosenberg, Bernard, and Fliegel, Norris. *The Vanguard Artist.* Chicago: Quadrangle, 1965.

Rosenberg, Harold. *The Tradition of the New.* New York: McGraw-Hill, 1965.

Rossi, Alice. "A Biosocial Perspective on Parenting." *Daedalus,* Vol. 106, No. 2 (1977).

————. "Contemporary American Feminism: In and Out of the Political Mainstream." Paper delivered to an International Symposium on Research on Popular Movements, Stockholm, Sweden, Feb. 7, 1978.

————, ed. *The Feminist Papers.* New York: Bantam, 1974.

————and Calderwood, Ann, eds. *Academic Women on the Move.* New York: Russell Sage, 1973.

Rudick, Sara and Daniels, Pamela. *Working It Out.* New York: Pantheon, 1977.

Schickel, Richard. "The Movies are Now High Art." In David Manning White. *Pop Culture in America.* Chicago: Quadrangle, 1969, pp. 141-52.

Sennett, Richard. "Destructive Gemeinschaft." *Partisan Review,* Vol. 3 (1976).

Sitney, P. Adams, ed. *Visionary Film; the American Avant Garde.* New York: Oxford University Press, 1974.

————, ed. *Film Culture Reader.* New York: Praeger, 1970.

Sklar, Robert. *Movie-Made America.* New York: Random House, 1975.

Smith, Sharon. *Women Who Make Movies.* New York: Hopkinson and Blake, 1975.

Weber, Max. *The Theory of Social and Economic Organization.* New York: Oxford University Press, 1947.

Wolfe, Tom. "The 'Me' Decade and the Third Great Awakening." *New York Magazine,* Vol. 9 (Aug. 23, 1976).

Index